Creating PC Video

Douglas Stevenson
Robert Wolenik

Focal Press

Boston   Oxford   Auckland   Johannesburg   Melbourne   New Delhi

Focal Press is an imprint of Butterworth–Heinemann.

Copyright © 1999 by Butterworth–Heinemann

 A member of the Reed Elsevier group

 Recognizing the importance of preserving what has been written, Butterworth–Heinemann prints its books on acid-free paper whenever possible.

 Butterworth–Heinemann supports the efforts of American Forests and the Global ReLeaf program in its campaign for the betterment of trees, forests, and our environment.

Library of Congress Cataloging-in-Publication Data

Stevenson, Douglas, 1953–
    Creating PC video / Douglas Stevenson, Robert Wolenik.
       p.   cm.
    ISBN 0-240-80361-2 (alk. paper)
      1. Video tapes—Editing—Data processing.   2. Video recordings—
Production and direction—Data processing.   3. Digital video.
    I. Wolenik, Robert.   II. Title.
    TR899.S78   1999
    778.59'3—dc21   99-30436
                                       CIP

British Library Cataloguing-in-Publication Data

A catalogue record for this book is available from the British Library.
The publisher offers special discounts on bulk orders of this book.
For information, please contact:

    Manager of Special Sales
    Butterworth–Heinemann
    225 Wildwood Avenue
    Woburn, MA 01801-2041
    Tel: 781-904-2500
    Fax: 781-904-2620

For information on all Focal Press publications available, contact our World Wide Web home page at: http://www.focalpress.com

10 9 8 7 6 5 4 3 2 1

Printed in the United States of America

CREDITS

Contents

Preface

It can happen to you, because it happened to us. In less than ten years, we have gone from our first, full-sized VHS camcorder to a full-time video production company based around a nonlinear editing system. What started out as a simple interest in family memories has been transformed by a trek down the path to better and better quality video productions, a series of choices that has changed our lives and careers.

The message is this: The opportunity is there. Your camcorder and computer have video potential limited only by your desires and imagination. From animation to documentaries, vacation videos to broadcast television, the marriage of the PC to video is a match made in heaven, a connecting link to your creative soul.

My first camcorder was a full-sized RCA VHS, one of the first with a flying erase head. I began shooting and learning about composition, simple editing, and videoing children, relatives, and special events.

The real challenge was editing. Using my camcorder as a source machine and a home VCR as a recorder, we discovered by trial and error how to create simple videos without a lot of equipment. About then we got the serious bug. We were having fun, and the dream of producing our own videos was glimmering off on the horizon. We wanted more.

At first the computer was strictly a word processor. A few years later it became an indispensable tool for titles and special effects as well as the foundation of a new business in video. Faster than we could imagine, the computer became the very heart and soul of all our video production. With it we can match speeds with the top production houses in the big city, accomplishing tasks that even they could not accomplish only a few short years ago.

Just as suddenly, video no longer simply meant tape and television. New formats such as CD-ROM and the Internet now consume almost as much of our attention as productions destined for tape. Digital video is redefining not only how but where we see and use video.

The purpose of this book is to open the door to the world of PC video. Multifaceted, ever changing, challenging your technical abilities as well as your creative instincts, the convergence of video and the computer can be as simple as a country road and as fast moving as a rocket to the moon. Get ready for a fun ride.

Although the price and capability of hardware may change and versions of software are continually upgraded, the basic concepts behind setting up and using an A/V computer for the most part remain will the same. For this reason we keep the information in each chapter general rather than refer to specific brand names. At the end of this book, you will find an appendix that gives examples of hardware and software to consider and the applications for which they are used. These are but a sampling of what is available, however we endeavor to include most of the primary players in the industry. It is our hope that this will point you in the right direction.

Producer, director, shooter, editor, narrator, actor, animator, music maker—how many hats can one person wear? First, you must believe in yourself. Take things one step at a time, acquiring the necessary tools and hardware, skills, and talents. Before you know it, you'll be amazed at how far you've come.

The Camcorder–Computer Link

1

When camcorders were first introduced to consumers well over a decade ago, there was no video hobby field. There were no prosumers. There were only broadcast professionals.

The reasons for this were both technical and economic. The equipment to handle postproduction work (refining the video after it's shot) was sophisticated and difficult to use. Typically it cost in the hundreds of thousands of dollars. Very few were likely to pop for that kind of money just so they could have fun making videos. While wonderful titles, special effects, even primitive morphing regularly could be seen on television, in no way could home users attempt it.

Yet, even in the early days, with well over a million camcorders sold a year (current there are closer to 3.5 million sold each year), there was a definite demand for equipment that could at the least do simple editing. And very quickly such tools became available.

THE STAND-ALONES

Stand-alones essentially are black boxes that can perform basic tasks. Among the first were simple editors from companies such as Videonics and Sima. These early machines, often difficult to manipulate, would allow the user to hobble together scenes and even add a couple of wipes and titles. They were primitive, but at the time everyone was excited to have them.

After all, up until then, the basic method of creating a video outside a broadcast studio was "crash editing." Here you played back the tape in the camcorder and recorded it to a VCR attempting to edit scenes by pushing the Pause/Record buttons at appropriate times. Needless to say things didn't always work out smoothly.

Later, companies such as FutureVideo introduced edit controllers, which allowed the user to create an EDL (edit decision list) and automated the basic editing procedures. Soon these included TBCs (time base correctors) to avoid glitches in the video. Separate title makers and simple effects generators (creating a variety of wipes) also were introduced. The home hobbyist could create a video that exceeded the performance of what previously could be done on film, but it still was a far cry from what was happening on broadcast. Today black box editing remains an effective and inexpensive way of getting into postproduction. Except, modern machines are more powerful, easier to use, and less expensive.

ENTER THE COMPUTER

What about all those wonderful effects that can be seen in science fiction and other movies? Can these, too, be done at home?

Yes, and it all began largely with the introduction of one machine, the Video Toaster by NewTek at the end of the 1980s. The Video Toaster used an Amiga computer as its base and allowed any user to create all sorts of mixing and effects (some even better than what regularly was seen on television) for the then unheard of price of under $10,000 (under $5,000 for the basic system). Suddenly, the world of video changed. The introduction of computer-based postproduction made equipment, if not necessarily simpler to use, certainly much more effective and sophisticated.

While the Video Toaster reigned supreme for nearly five years (it was so good it was even used to create special effects on many television shows), it eventually was superseded by a wide variety of programs that could create virtually anything in video on both Macintosh and Wintel platforms.

Stand-alone products continued to increase in quality as well as work with digital mixers (allowing true A/B rolls, also called dissolves) introduced by Videonics and a host of other superhigh-quality character generators and effects machines. Most of these cost under $2,000.

Bigger advances, however, came about on the computer side. Soon a host of programs, often costing under a $1,000, were available to handle editing of scenes, adding titles, creating wipes, and much more. There were even morphing programs that could duplicate, albeit much slower, almost any effect seen in the sci-fi movies.

With the introduction of computers it became possible, at relatively little cost, albeit slower, to do anything at home that could be done in the broadcast studio. As a result, a new breed of videographer emerged.

THE EVENT VIDEOGRAPHER

Since the first camcorders were introduced in the 1980s, people had been using them to record weddings, bar mitzvahs, family events, and so on. Usually these were strictly amateur (that is, without pay) efforts. While a "true photographer" might be hired to take photographs or even film a short movie of the event, an amateur videographer friend or relative might supplement the memory-capturing with a video.

However, that changed when two things became clear: First, through the use of the Hi8 and Super VHS formats, videos could be taken that were just as clear as the old Super8 movie films. Second, through the use of the Video Toaster, digital mixer, and later computerized programs, postproduction techniques could rival those of the professionals.

Suddenly that amateur, who previously would simply record a wedding and then turn a copy over to the family, could edit the tape, blending scenes, adding music, titles, wipes, and more. In short, the wedding tape became a real video production, something of true value, something people were willing to pay for. Thus was born the event videographer, a person who could charge, often high amounts, for videotaping an event, initially mostly weddings.

Today, most events that are significant enough to warrant a photographer, also warrant a videographer. Indeed, with the development of still video allowing individual shots to be pulled from camcorders, the videographer can supersede the photographer, in short be all that's required.

THE WORLD TURNED DIGITAL

While it may seem that the blending of camcorders with computers was a happy marriage, initially it was not. There was a huge problem. Camcorders, although basically digital instruments, recorded onto videotape in an analog format. (VHS, S-VHS, 8mm, and Hi8 are all analog formats.) On the other hand, computers were digital instruments. They understood only the world of ones and zeros.

Getting the video shot with a camcorder into the computer so it could be manipulated (not just simply played on the monitor, which could be done with a simple capture card) required the use of a digitizing board. In the mid-1990s the big scramble was to come up with computer boards that could take that analog signal, convert it to digital, and after it had been manipulated by the computer, convert it back to analog for recording onto videotape. The first computerized video studios essentially were hybrids—analog and digital combined.

This produced some unwanted results. Every time a scene in an analog format is copied onto videotape, some of it is lost. Make four generations of copies (a copy of a copy of a copy of a copy) and even Hi8 or Super VHS is unwatchable.

Using a hybrid system allowed postproduction work to be done making only three or (in some cases) two generations. But, it was still only a work-around solution that really wasn't satisfactory. A pure digital system, from camcorder to computer, was needed.

THEN CAME FIREWIRE

Such a system became possible in the late 1990s with the introduction of FireWire (1384 protocol). This system allowed computers to connect digitally with a wide variety of peripherals, including camcorders. At the same time, camcorders were introduced that recorded digitally onto a tiny cassette. The new DVC (digital videocassette) format was capable of up to 500 lines of horizontal resolution (100 better than Hi8 or S-VHS).

Initially, very few of the new digital format camcorders had a FireWire port allowing them to link directly with computers. However, that changed after a couple of years, when virtually all digital camcorders had the port. Today, almost any digital camcorder can play back in digital format directly to a computer. As a result, there is no generational loss when getting into postproduction.

A NEW WORLD OF HARD DRIVES

Another development that occurred in the late 1990s was the introduction of superfast, superlarge hard drives. In the early years of computers, storing video on a hard drive was impractical. Only a few seconds of video would require megabytes of storage. A minute or less would fill up an old hard drive. Therefore, a hybrid storage system, using the old analog tape, was necessary. A few seconds of video would be pumped into the computer, manipulated, then sent back to the tape and another few seconds pumped—an awkward and inefficient system at best.

However, the introduction of multigigabyte hard drives and RAID systems changed all that. Suddenly 10, 20, 80, or more gigabytes of storage could be made available, at remarkably low prices, often only a few thousand dollars. Further, these were true A/V drives with fast throughput speeds. (They could record the video as it was played without dropping frames.)

Suddenly it was possible to have a true digital editing system from camcorder to storage. Record digitally, transfer the entire scene (many minutes, sometimes as much as an hour's worth) directly into the computer, manipulate it inside, and then store it digitally either on a removable hard drive or, as an alternative, on a CD or later a DVD. The only time it was necessary to transfer to analog tape was to create a copy to sell to someone.

Better computers, with blistering speeds of 500 MHz and higher and huge amounts of RAM approaching 1,000 MB, made all of this work even better. The day of the "home" postproduction studio arrived.

This is not to say that, as this is written, there are no problems. Artifacts sometimes crop up in the video. Software often doesn't work easily (or sometimes not at all) with the hardware. Some programs are difficult to use and don't do all that they promise. (We'll look at these throughout this book.) Yet, basically the world of the inexpensive editing suite that a person can use for hobby or business is here.

You don't have to be a computer whiz or have a degree in cinematography from a major university to break into video. You can do it on a small scale, a step at a time. You can start with a camcorder and some basic black box equipment. As your experience and knowledge grow (and perhaps as you recoup some of your investment from selling your video services), you can expand your equipment. That's what we'll show you how to do in the next chapters.

Selecting the Right Camcorder

2

Whether you are about to purchase your first camcorder or are ready to upgrade your old clunker for a sleek new model, it pays to know what you are looking for. Although the basics of camcorder design have not really changed all that much over the years, the camcorder on the shelf today has many night-and-day differences from its brethren of yesteryear. So before you plunk down some serious cash or some heavy-duty plastic to go home with the camcorder of your dreams, let's explore what to look for and which features are essential for any home videographer with an interest in desktop video.

WHICH FORMAT IS RIGHT FOR YOU?

No one wants to look at a picture that is out of focus or in black and white when it is supposed to be in full color. We expect our images to be as good as possible, clear, sharp, and with perfect hue. If money were no object we'd all like the best; and when it comes to camcorders, it is clear that the very highest picture quality comes from the latest digital camcorders. Approaching video quality levels comparable to commercial broadcast's Betacam SP, the DVC format (Table 2–1) has set a new standard for clarity and resolution. Colors are more accurate. Hues are full without being oversaturated and bleeding beyond their edges. As the digital format becomes more established, many things become possible. Image perfection is maintained due to digital's ability to compare and replicate pixel content, eliminating many dropouts and other imperfections. The camcorder immediately is directly compatible with the computer, through the new FireWire connection.

Of course, not everyone can afford or wants to spend the extra bucks for digital. The logical choice becomes Hi8, a format that uses 8mm-size tapes but processes the video at a slightly higher resolution than regular 8mm, VHS, or VHS-C.

Table 2–1. Comparison of Formats

Quality Rating	Format	Horizontal Resolution	Tape Size	Signal
1	Betacam SP	500+	1/2 inch	Component
2	DVC	500	6mm (1/4 inch)	Digital/component recording
3	Hi8	400	8mm	"S"
3	S-VHS	400	1/2 inch	"S"
4	3/4 inch SP	280	3/4 inch	Composite plus a dub mode
5	3/4 inch	250	3/4 inch	Composite
6	8mm	250	8mm	Composite
6	VHS	250	1/2 inch	Composite

The Hi8 (and S-VHS) format uses as system known as Y/C processing, electronic circuits that take the information from the CCD and use it to put together the final video image. Unlike standard composite video, which combines all video information together, Y/C works by keeping the luminance or contrast (black-and-white) portion of the signal separate from the chrominance (color signal). Both Hi8 and digital camcorders provide a special "S" connector (Figure 2–1) for a Y/C video output signal, which can be sent to a compatible TV or VCR.

S-VHS is a format, introduced several years ago, utilizing the same Y/C processing as Hi8, but in a VHS tape format. In the consumer marketplace, S-VHS lost to Hi8 but established a foothold in industrial and commercial circles. Although some models still are available, the superiority of digital over Hi8 and S-VHS leaves the future of both in doubt.

Figure 2–1. Comparison of video cables: RCA/phono, BNC, and "S." Video cables come in a variety of configurations, including (from right to left) the RCA or phono connector; the BNC, found in industrial video applications; and the Y/C connector, which keeps contrast and color signals on separate pins.

For the camcorder shopper it's often a matter of deciding, "Yes, I will spend the extra money for this feature and format to achieve higher resolution." But the choice goes a little beyond that. Because the manufacturer knows you are willing to pay more for a better picture, quite often other factors that contribute to better image quality, such as the CCD pixel count, are incorporated into the design of more expensive camcorders.

Why spend the money for higher resolution? A primary benefit of Y/C or digital processing becomes apparent to the end user during the process of editing. The loss of resolution that happens when you drop down a generation to create an edited master tape is less with a Y/C or digital format than with standard 8mm or VHS, because the original footage starts out with a significantly better picture.

Many of the TVs on the market today will accept a Y/C signal directly from your camcorder. Even if your TV is not equipped with the special Y/C or "S" connector and processing, a standard composite video signal originally recorded on a Y/C or digital format will be noticeably better than the image of regular VHS or 8mm.

THREE-CHIP VIDEO QUALITY

Even among digital camcorders, there are different levels of quality. The biggest distinction is in the number of CCDs or image processing chips. Almost all camcorders today use a single CCD for image processing, taking what comes out of the lens and turning it into what we see on a TV. The best resolution and color accuracy today comes from camcorders that use three video chips or CCDs (Figure 2–2) to convert the light passing through the lens into the electrical signals that become the video. Modeled after professional cameras used in broadcast circles, three-chip processing divides the image into separate signals of red, green, and blue (RGB). Perhaps some day engineers will figure out how to achieve equal results with single-chip processing, but until that day the superiority of three chips, with their greater surface area and more precise color reproduction, is undisputed.

Of course, this extra quality comes at a price, adding a thousand dollars or more to the cost of your camcorder. Is the expense worth it? For the average videographer, probably not. However for those with professional aspirations, that is, those with plans to get paid for their video services or

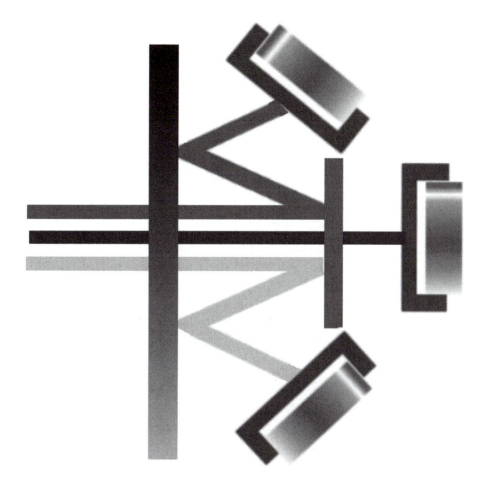

Figure 2–2. Three-chip configuration (see color insert). Most camcorders use a single CCD after the camcorder lens to process the video signal. A three-chip system provides more accurate color by dividing the color signal into three components: red, green, and blue (RGB).

produce special interest videos for resale, achieving maximum resolution and color accuracy should be a high priority. If you can afford the extra bucks or if you have any plans to use your camcorder for any professional work, be it weddings, real estate, or local sporting events, don't hesitate to go the extra mile for a three-chip camcorder.

THE SMALLER, THE BETTER

What is the optimum size for a camcorder? Without denying the greater stability of a full-size camcorder that rests on your shoulder, electronic image stabilization, common on most small camcorders, has pretty much eliminated that problem. When it comes time to go on a vacation, family outing, or to some other special event, will you think twice before dragging the camcorder along? Are you the tourist nerd with a big camera bag at your side, lugging it through airports and scenic tours, embarrassing your family with this constant piece of luggage at your side?

There's something to be said for the old axiom, Small is beautiful. Imagine a camcorder that you could slip in a shirt or jacket pocket, whip out for video snapshots, then return discreetly out of sight until the next video photo-op. It's here (see Figure 2–3). Some of the latest digital camcorders have made some amazing strides in size reduction. Granted, the

Figure 2–3. Sony digital camcorder model DCR-PC10. Today's camcorders come in increasingly smaller packages.

professional videographer looking for a piece of equipment suitable for weddings or the production of special interest videos will have a different set of desires and parameters. However, for the casual camcorder owner who wants a video tool for home movies, convenience is king.

MANUAL OPTIONS

Nothing says amateur video like a tape that is constantly going in and out of focus. Instead of watching the subject on camera, your attention is distracted by a picture that gets fuzzy, then clear, then fuzzy, then clear again. Autofocus systems react to movement and the proximity or distance of the subject from the camcorder. While extremely useful, it can be just as useful to have the option of turning off the autofocus.

A similar problem can be experienced with the camcorder's auto-iris function. A subject with a white shirt can cause the iris to close down a bit too far, making the person's face dark. Changing lighting conditions, even small things such as the person turning to present the camcorder with more or less white surface area, will make the iris open and close, resulting in a picture that gets repeatedly brighter and darker, another distraction. Turning off the auto mechanism and using a manual control, the iris could be opened slightly, just enough to make the face brighter and more visible, without washing out the detail on the shirt, holding steady despite subtle shifts in lighting.

The vast majority of camcorders today have been stripped of all manual controls, simply because most people never touch them. They simply point and shoot and expect the camcorder to do the rest—and it will, to a large degree. It's just that, if you want to take the extra steps to make your videos as good as they can be, manual control always is better than full auto. At least you want to have the manual option there when it's appropriate.

While we're at it, we can add white balance to the list of desirable manual features. This helps you get your colors as accurate as possible. Because we shoot in so many different types of lighting, from indoor incandescence and fluorescence to bright sun or cloudy days out of doors, the camcorder's ability to white balance or make color adjustments is very important. Some camcorders give you a semi-manual white balance option by providing a way for you to tell your camcorder, through an adjustment wheel, whether you're shooting outdoors or inside, on a cloudy day or in bright light. Accurate colors mean better images and video that is more pleasing to the eye.

The option is called *white balance* because white is the reference color. Just as with a prism, white has a relationship to all other colors. In real life our mind has the ability to adjust our eyes for different types of lighting so that colors maintain their natural hues. Today's camcorders make the same judgment calls, determining the amount and quality (color temperature) of the light passing through the lens, doing its best to deliver colors accurately to the videotape or screen. As the amount of light present in the scene decreases, the camcorder and its white balance circuitry have a more difficult time maintaining proper hues. Video often gains a reddish or greenish tint. Even the best camera requires adequate lighting to perform up to expectations.

A camcorder with manual white balance adjusted to a reference color almost always will deliver the most accurate hues. To set the manual white balance, you aim the camcorder at a white surface such as a large piece of poster board, a shirt, or a white wall, anything large enough for you to fill the screen completely. Next you press a button on the camcorder that tells the white balance circuitry on the inside, "Check this out, this is supposed to be white." Once this white reference has been established, the camcorder knows what to do with the rest of the colors to balance things accordingly.

POWER TO SPARE

Probably the single biggest change for camcorders in recent years is in battery power. Virtually all manufacturers have left nicad batteries behind in favor of lithium-powered cells. Why? Because unlike nicads, which eventually lose their ability to take a charge, lithium batteries always charge to maximum capacity no matter what their discharge level is at the beginning. Let's make that a little clearer. With nicad batteries, let's say you record for an hour and when you're finished, the battery is discharged by about 50%. You put it on the charger and bring it back up to full power. The next time you use your camcorder after an hour goes by instead of being discharged about 50%, you discover your battery is completely drained. In real life, this so-called memory effect doesn't happen overnight, but gradually you'll find that your camcorder nicad batteries have less and less charge life and eventually no longer accept a charge and you must buy new ones.

Today's high-capacity lithium batteries have absolutely no memory effect, no matter how much you discharge or how often you charge them. You'll also find they have greater capacity than ever before, delivering up to several hours of recording time, setting an incredible new standard for longevity and power.

Add a touch of microprocessor technology, and your battery can tell exactly how much charge it has left. Built in to some new models is a battery power meter. More than a simple bar graph estimate, the power meter is accurate to within plus or minus 1 minute.

Improvements also have been made in how long it takes to charge your batteries. Quick-charging systems can give your spent batteries enough power for 1 hour of operation in only 15 minutes. An LCD readout continually lets you see how much power or recording time has been added.

Another extra you'll find in various models of camcorders is the battery shell that holds standard AA batteries. No place or time to recharge your batteries? In an emergency you can run for up to 2 hours on six AA batteries, so you'll always have power for any situation.

ZOOOOOM

Its not uncommon to see an optical (that is, the glass lens) with a 16 or 18 to 1 ratio, with some models sporting an incredible range of 22 to 1. This means that the magnification at maximum telephoto position is 22 times greater than the extreme wide-angle position. Greater optical range gives you more flexibility when framing a subject and the ability to get a decent closeup on a subject a pretty good distance away.

Zoom ranges are extended even further through digital technology, doubling, even quadrupling, the optical magnification. The image in digital form is examined, and calculated extrapolations add in extra pixels to increase the size of the subject beyond the physical magnification of the lens. When used properly to the casual observer the image looks clear and certainly very much enlarged. However, some systems take the digital enhancement to an extreme, until the image loses quality and clarity. In the right hands, the benefits of the digital zoom cannot be denied and it can be a very desirable feature.

VARIABLE-SPEED ZOOM

One more feature that relates to the zoom could be considered one of the most important features to look for, yet it is found on only a limited number of camcorder models: the variable speed zoom. Most camcorders come with a single-speed zoom. Press the zoom rocker arm or switch, and the lens moves in or out at a fixed speed, usually fast or moderately fast. This is interesting, since you really want your zoom speed to be slow or slower. A fast zoom says, "Hey look at me! I'm zooming." Instead your zoom should be almost transparent or invisible. The zoom or pullback should be so gentle and smooth that the viewer doesn't realize it's happening, only that the subject is easier to see or that more background is coming into view.

Some camcorders today have two- and three-speed zooms: slow, medium, and fast. Press on the zoom switch lightly and you get the first, slowest speed. Press a little harder and the zoom motor changes gears. Press all the way and you have the fastest speed, to be used when you must frame up a shot in a hurry. If the camcorder's slow is the right speed, this often is sufficient.

Better still are the variable-speed zooms, whose speed is directly proportional to the amount of pressure on or position of the switch. It can take a little trial and error to get the feel of the relationship of speed to pressure or position, but once you get it down, you'll find their operation to be second nature. A variable- or a multispeed zoom is a major step up from a single speed, one that will greatly enhance your creative capabilities.

COLOR MONITORS AND COLOR VIEWFINDERS

Color monitors, the large foldout LCD screens (Figure 2–4), give you a much larger viewing area when shooting and can be angled, enabling you to hold the camcorder over your head or down at your waist and still have a good view of your subject. They also function as an excellent playback monitor with built-in speaker, so that reviewing the day's recording is as easy as rewinding your tape. Better still, everyone who can crowd around the little screen gets to watch your recording.

The standard electronic viewfinders still have their place. The larger LCD screens can get washed out in bright sunlight and then you have to switch back to the old reliable. Most camcorders with large LCD monitor

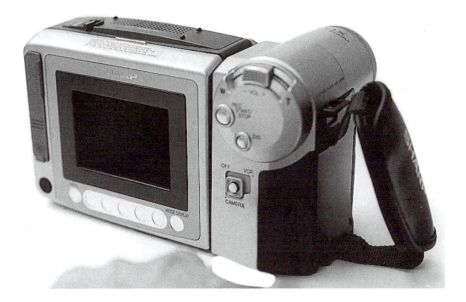

Figure 2–4. Camcorder with LCD monitor.

screens have black-and-white electronic viewfinders (EVFs). These still work fine, in fact the black-and-white EVF screens make it easy to see image detail clearly.

Many camcorders today without a foldout monitor often have color viewfinders. These are nice, too, having greatly improved in sharpness and color clarity over the last few years. There is a certain appeal to seeing your recordings much as they will appear when displayed on a TV. In the end, foldout monitor, color EVF, or regular black and white all will work fine, so what appeals to you is what counts.

ELECTRONIC IMAGE STABILIZATION

Electronic image stabilization (EIS) is getting to be so standard on palm-sized camcorders that it almost seems redundant to mention it—except that it isn't. Every camcorder today does not have image stabilization, particularly some entry-level, low-priced units. However, EIS does so much to make handheld video worth watching that no one should ever, ever buy a (palm-sized) camcorder without it. There are times when it should be turned off, such as when the camcorder is mounted on a tripod, but again it's not handheld then. You'll find that the vast majority of family home video is shot handheld, and a stabilized picture can make the difference between seasick shake and downright good video.

There are two types of EIS: The optical type works by a sort of gyro-scope mechanism on the lens; the digital type does it all through pixel magic. The optical (Figure 2–5) EIS people claim superiority, since digital processing is inherently not as pure as unadulterated optical video. Chances are your audience won't know which EIS system your camcorder has, as long as you use it.

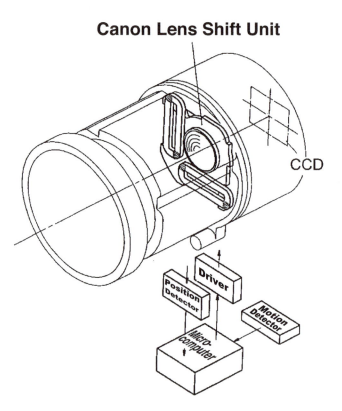

Canon Lens Shift Unit

Figure 2–5. Canon lens unit with EIS. Image stabilization circuits take the shake out of handheld camera work.

1. Canon lens structure with no camera shake

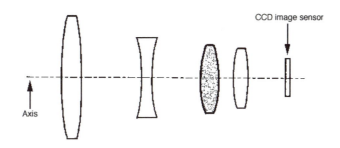

2. Lens front shakes downward

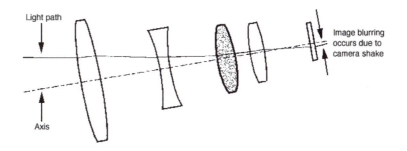

3. Lens shift, counteracting downward camera shake, redirects light path and cancels out shake

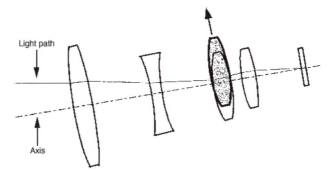

Figure 2–5. (continued).

EXTERNAL MICROPHONE AND HEADPHONE JACKS

Every camcorder comes with a built-in camera mike. This will get the job done, but often the difference between a good video and great video is not the picture but the sound. Stand at the back of a room and shoot someone speaking from, say, 20 or 30 feet away. You can see them, you even can zoom in so that the person's face fills the screen, but his or her voice is lost or sounds like it's coming from of a deep hole. Contrast that image with one that has full clear sound and the difference will seem like night and day.

The use of an external (remote or wireless) mike can be extremely beneficial in a number of situations. At a wedding the bride and groom almost always will virtually whisper their vows to one another. In this situation you are always a good distance away from your subjects. The clergy usually has a booming voice that carries well, but picking up the voices of the bride and groom is almost impossible. Consider the difference a wireless mike, placed inconspicuously on the groom, can make. Suddenly the intimacy of the moment comes alive. There won't be a dry eye in your audience.

Many people like to use a camcorder to interview elderly family members, gathering history and stories for future generations. The difference between a microphone that is 5 or 6 feet away and one placed on the person (a lapel mike) is very dramatic. You transform the sound from audible but weak to warm and full. We are used to this level of quality from watching television, especially interview and talk shows. The simple addition of the lapel mike makes all the difference.

When comparing camcorders, you'll find that actually very few today have the jack for connecting an external microphone. This is understandable from the manufacturer's point of view, since the vast majority of people never take that extra step to purchase an external microphone. However if you consider your camcorder a tool you plan to use for years and years to come, it is nice to have the option of adding a mike when or if you ever decide to make it part of your kit.

The other side of the coin is the headphone jack. Again, many or most of today's camcorders do not include a way for you to connect headphones for monitoring sound. You wouldn't consider recording without a viewfinder. Taping without listening to the sound is the audio equivalent. Headphones let you know exactly what sound is going onto your tape and, in an interview situation, that can be valuable information to have.

EDIT CONTROL

To ease the task of editing and make it fun, it helps to have a camcorder that provides for external control. Your computer can function as an edit controller, allowing you to use your camcorder as either the source or record deck. From your keyboard, play tapes and digitize them to the computer hard drive or play edited projects from the computer and record them to a master tape in your camcorder. Properly connected, you can use the computer mouse to operate your camcorder's VCR functions like Play, Fast Forward, Pause, and even Jog/Shuttle.

One style of interface is the Control L or LANC connector. Located on the outside of the camcorder, it links the camcorder to the computer/edit controller via a hardwired cable. A few camcorder manufacturers have proprietary multipin edit control connectors or control the camcorder through infrared signals. Digital camcorder owners have an advantage here. The Firewire connection not only passes audio and video signals, it can control your camcorder's playback functions as well. If you plan to use your camcorder and computer for editing, be sure not to overlook this important feature.

SUMMARY

Selecting the right camcorder is a matter of making an informed decision (Figure 2–6) based on your needs and pocketbook. Fortunately there are plenty to choose from, all of which will give you years of great service and are valuable and essential tools for desktop video.

Manufacturer: _____

Model: _____

Suggested retail price: _____

Size and weight: _____

Format—digital, Y/C (Hi8, S-VHS), 8mm, or VHS? _____

CCDs—three chip or single chip? _____

Image sensor pixel count: _____

Manual focus? _____

Manual iris? _____

Manual white balance? _____

Battery power: _____

Microphone input? _____

Headphone output?_____

Multispeed zoom? _____

Variable-speed zoom? _____

Maximum zoom-lens power: _____

LCD monitor? _____

Color viewfinder? _____

Electronic image stabilization? _____

Edit control connection? _____

A/V in? _____

Figure 2–6. Camcorder features checklist.

Computer Video Options for Under $500

3

What does it take to set up a home computer for video? That's a big question, with more than a dozen answers. The marketplace is flooded with choices, and to determine which route is the one for you takes a little education, enabling you to make an informed decision. You must begin by asking yourself, "What do I want from my system?" Frame capture of still images? Video editing? The ability to e-mail video movies or play them on a website? Because the marketplace offers so many different products with just as wide a range of price tags and capabilities, it is important for the person in search of a computer video system to examine the capabilities and claims of each product closely, lest your purchase falls short of your expectations.

COMPUTER CONTROLLED TAPE-TO-TAPE EDITING

To keep prices low, there has to be some element of compromise. Every second of video from your camcorder is composed of 30 separate frames, which when it comes right down to it are really nothing more than sequential still images. Examined individually and uncompressed, each frame can be as much as a half to a full megabyte or more in size. Unless you go the big bucks route with dedicated video hard drives, you or your software must follow an alternate route.

A common approach taken by a few software developers is to use the computer as an edit controller and tool for generating an edit decision list. Actual editing still is done from tape to tape; that is, the original tape masters from your camcorder are recorded to what will be an edited tape in a VCR, with the computer controlling playback and recording operations for both machines. If your final goal is a videotape you can play on your home VCR and TV, this technique gives you the best-quality video you can expect from a low-priced consumer editing system. The camcorder is connected to the computer via an edit control cable, with either a Control L (LANC) or Panasonic five-pin connection. Another option is for the camcorder and VCR to be controlled through an infrared emitter, a device that sends out infrared signals to control playback and other VCR type functions, just like a remote control.

VIDEO CAPTURE

The other approach is to record or digitize your camcorder video directly to the standard hard drive in your computer. To accomplish this, your software must compress the video to a size your computer can handle. Screen dimensions typically are reduced from the full-screen 640 × 480 pixels to 320 × 240 pixels (Figure 3–1A) or smaller, such as 160 × 120 pixels (Figure 3–1B). The video signal itself is run through compression algorithms that remove redundant pixels and apply other digital wizardry to make the final file size as small as possible. These reduced-sized screens have their applications, such as for CD-ROMs, the Internet, or playback directly from the hard drive. All these multimedia formats are limited in the amount of information they can process per second and require that your video files be as small as possible. However, since these mediums constitute a major outlet

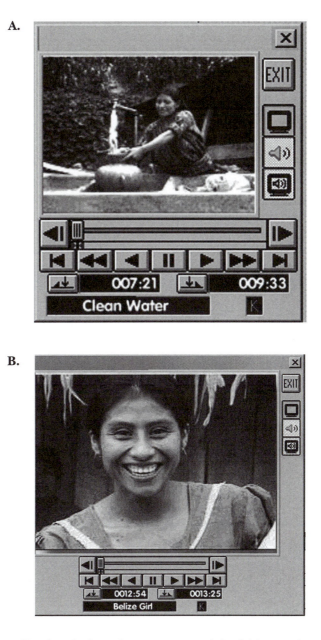

Figure 3–1. Samples of screen size. To reduce the demands on your computer's hard drive capacity, screen dimensions for digitized video typically are reduced from the full-screen 640 × 480 pixels to 320 × 240 (B) pixels or smaller (A, 160 × 120).

for video productions, the necessary compromise and video file reductions make perfect sense.

Grabbing Frames

Quite often many computer projects really only require a single frame of video, essentially a photo but from a video source. Commonly known as a *frame grabber,* your hardware–software combination (Figure 3–2) can capture a single video frame and send it to the hard drive memory. This screen image then can be imported into any of a variety of programs. In an art program you can reduce it in size, crop or cut away unnecessary background, add a title, adjust the brightness and contrast, or modify the color. You can save the image as a bitmap, .tif, or Internet-friendly file type such as a .jpeg or .gif.

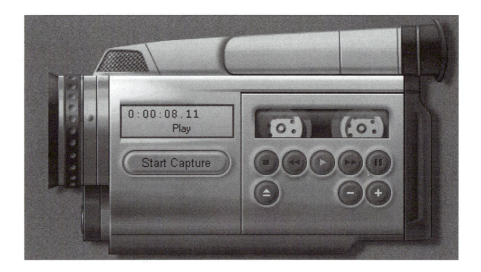

Figure 3–2. Video frame capture software screen. Turn your video into a still image with a frame capture program and associated hardware.

Frame capture can be done at various resolution settings. Higher resolution can produce a picture with greater detail but requires a larger file size. While full-screen video is represented as 640 × 480 pixels, an image half as large (at 320 × 240 pixels) is a closer approximation of a typical photo, requiring much less space on your hard drive. Each video card carries different specifications regarding the resolution it can process for video and frame capture. Examine the specs carefully when making a buying decision.

Video Capture Cards, Internal and External

Probably one of the biggest distinctions in hardware is whether you use an internally mounted video capture card (Figure 3–3A) or go for the style hardware that works outside the computer (Figure 3–3B). Internal cards generally mount in a PCI slot on the motherboard of the computer. The card extends to the rear of the computer, where connections for the video input and output signals are exposed. The advantage of the internal card is that it does not require its own power supply but draws its electricity from the power supply inside the computer. It also makes for a more compact installation, with one less piece of hardware around your computer setup. Probably the biggest question you have to answer is, "Do you have an available PCI slot?" As more and more hardware devices, such as scanners and Zip drives and associated cards, vie for your computer's available slots, you have to make sure there is an open slot for the video capture card.

External devices are the perfect solution for home computer owners who'd just as soon not venture inside the mysterious realm under the cover. Most external video devices plug into the computer's parallel port; however, this spot too often is occupied by some other piece of hardware, such as a printer. Fortunately parallel ports are designed to be shared. Devices that use parallel ports allow the computer's connections to be looped through and passed on to feed other pieces of hardware in a chain.

Making the right connections can just be the first step in getting your video capture system up and running. It may be necessary to adjust the computer's internal BIOS settings, accomplished through on-screen commands.

A.

B.

Figure 3–3. Video capture options: (A) In-board video cards fit into a PCI slot on your computer's mother-board, (B) Out-board systems give you all the function and capability without the need to go inside your computer.

ADDING AUDIO

When it comes to home productions, video usually is only half the equation. You also have to think about audio. Video capture cards with a price of $500 or less are for working strictly with video. For sound you need an audio card. Most computers these days come with an audio card, although in various levels of quality and features. All audio cards have outputs to connect with your external (powered or self-amplified) speakers, and generally speaking all have input connections, specifically Line In, where you would connect the audio output of a camcorder, tape, or CD player. Usually you'll have a microphone input as well, a more sensitive connection than the Line level connection, used for recording a voice directly to the hard drive. Cards compatable with FireWire pass both video and audio through a single digital connection, however, they will be a bit more expensive.

CHOOSING SOFTWARE

Just about any video capture card you consider comes with its own software. You must have a software interface to capture frames or live video (Figure 3–4) if you want to do any kind of editing.

Although screen size may be limited, the editing software on these inexpensive systems can be nearly as sophisticated as their high-end non-linear counterparts. Typically there are two forms of editing, storyboard and timeline, and in a way they are very similar. Storyboard editing (Figure 3–5) works with "thumbnail" or miniature single-frame representations of your digital video clips. You drag the clips from a library or collection of digitized video files to the storyboard and arrange them in any order. You get an instant idea of the progression of scenes and the story your video will tell.

Timeline editing (Figure 3–6) represents the progress of a scene in minutes and, depending on the scale, seconds or some other division of a minute. The timeline commonly will be divided into various tracks. The video clip track usually comes first and below that are tracks for audio (music, narration) and perhaps other tracks for titles or other graphics.

Just as in systems costing hundreds of dollars more, these simple editors have all the important features. For example, playback VCR-type

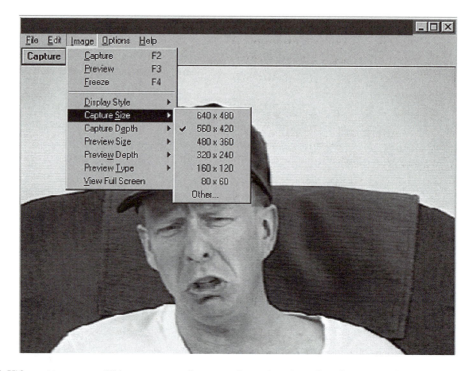

Figure 3–4. Video capture screen. Video capture cards use a software interface when digitizing video to your computer's hard drive.

Figure 3–5. Storyboard editing. Storyboard editing uses single images to represent scenes of your video.

Figure 3–6. Timeline editing. Timelines show the progression of your project in minutes and seconds.

buttons let you review the content of individual digitized clips. You can "trim," adjust the in and out points from the digitized scene, keeping only the section you want. Time counters tell you the length of the scene. It is all very intuitive and easy. Before you know it, you'll be editing like a pro.

ADDING TITLES

Some systems start you out with a library of preset titles (Figure 3–7), as well as allow you to create your own titles from scratch. Add an outline, a drop shadow, and change color or the color of the outline or shadow with the option of a gradient color fill. Change the font size, go bold, or italicize. It is amazing how sophisticated the character generator can be on such inexpensive software.

You'll be just as impressed at the number and high quality of the effects and transitions that can be yours. Start out with a basic fade or dissolve then cruise through other options like spiral wipes, flashy blinds, and more.

Some video capture programs are very basic, while others are extremely sophisticated. As mentioned earlier, because the editing software usually is bundled with the video card, it's a matter of becoming familiar with each program's capabilities before you buy.

MAKE A MOVIE

Ready to make a movie? Unless you have the tape to tape option, the movie you create will probably be saved as an .avi file. Because the digitized files are radically compressed and reduced in dimension from full screen (640 × 480 pixels) to only 320 × 240 or smaller, they really are not suitable for playback on a regular TV. They'll do fine played from your computer or e-mailed as an attachment on the Internet, since you want file sizes to be as small as possible anyway.

Another way to use your video on the Internet is with one of many video processing programs available. These systems use a technique called *streaming*, which sends the video file in real time from a website to the viewer's computer screen. We'll talk about this more in Chapter 9, "Video over the Internet."

Figure 3–7. Studio 400 titles. Pinnacle's Studio 400 series packs some powerful advanced editing features, including a collection of great looking titles, into an inexpensive package.

Eliminating frames also can reduce file size. The .avi video seen on the Internet or a CD-ROM may only have 15 frames per second rather than standard NTSC video's 30. Although this does "strobe" (that is, make the video look a bit jerky), overall content still is quite visible and acceptable. You'll find that some systems place a limit on the front end when you digitize, permitting only 15 frames a second to be captured to the hard drive.

BONUS—THE TV TUNER

A few video capture cards on the market add other features as well, sort of an added bonus. With the right hardware your computer can also function as a TV tuner. You can connect to cable or an outside antenna and catch your favorite shows in a resizable window or place the signal in the background while you continue to listen to the audio. It's a great way to stay up with the score on your favorite sport or stay abreast of a soap opera drama, while you work or surf the 'Net.

No matter which system you choose, you'll find the video capture card and its software a worthy investment, one that forms the bond between the camcorder and computer and brings desktop video to life.

Building the AV Computer

4

It is important here to begin drawing lines or defining what you expect to accomplish from your AV computer system. Will it be for creating edited home videos to play on your TV, miniature movies to e-mail over the Internet, or commercial productions for broadcast or industrial use? The budget for computer-based video editing varies from under $200 to well over $20,000 with many points in between. If playing video from your computer with images only a few inches across will make you happy, then just about any computer with a basic video and audio card will do. For full-screen reproduction that can be recorded back to tape and played in your VCR, you'll need to invest in a video card that can produce a 640 × 480 pixel image in composite, S-video, or for the best results, as a component (RGB) or a digital signal. If your goal is to produce videos for customers and clients, for resale as a special interest video, or to air on cable or broadcast television, then you'll want to make sure the hardware you select is up to the task.

SELECTING HARDWARE

The AV computer really comprises two separate sets of criteria: the hardware and the software. But you'll probably find that the computer and its associated hardware (Figure 4–1) will make up the bulk of the cost for a fully outfitted AV system. For a start, your computer needs to be as fast as possible, especially important for full-screen nonlinear editing. With nonlinear editing, the computer is required to manipulate huge amounts of data, and a computer with a greater clock speed simply can do your work faster. Even a 300 or 400 MHz system will give you plenty of opportunity to twiddle your thumbs or brew a new pot of coffee while you wait for your video images to be processed and rendered. This is the prime time to consider upgrading to a new computer. Basically you'll want to go as fast as you

Figure 4–1. The AV computer. Just about any computer will do. The associated hardware makes it an AV computer.

can afford plus install as much RAM as possible, more than twice what is needed for ordinary desktop applications such as a spreadsheet or a word processor. It's not uncommon to have 96, even 128 Megs of RAM or more in the typical computer outfitted for desktop video.

You'll spend the real bucks on the hard drive or hard drives. While prices for the average hard drive have come way down, these are no ordinary drives. Because the hard drive is the source for all your stored video, special "ultrafast and -wide" SCSI-controlled drives are used, which permit rapid access and processing of the video information. Even though most office computers usually have memory storage of 2–6 gigabytes, a healthy AV system requires at least 9 gigabytes, preferably a lot more. That's 9000 megabytes, what you'll need to store 15–20 minutes worth of video material—and create an edited production 5–10 minutes in length. Drive manufacturers boast tremendous amounts of storage time, but the real-life return seems to be about half of what their specs might claim. Obviously the more gigabytes of memory you have, the more video (and audio) can be stored in your computer. Computer video editors commonly chain together several drives in an "array" to build up a maximum of storage capacity. It's easy to spend $5,000 or more on the drives alone. The good news is prices on these video drives are dropping daily, falling by more than half in just the last couple of years. Manufacturers are now promoting 50-gigabyte drives that cost roughly the same as 9-gigabyte drives of only a few years ago.

NOW THE *BIG* QUESTION—HOW MUCH WILL IT COST?

If you're shooting for professional results, be ready to drop some cash. You'll find most of the popular entry-level professional systems start out at $8,000 (including the computer and multigigabyte drives) and go up from there. More good news is that prices are dropping fast and a number of new systems are breaking the price barriers, putting this sophisticated editing in the hands of more and more people. If you are willing to settle for less than broadcast quality, then some systems even are downright affordable, well under $1,000.

Often the prices you see quoted are just for the specific nonlinear hardware and software itself, since many people already own a computer. Even then, you'll find a wide price range on video cards, sound cards, and editing software. One thing for sure—before buying anything, take the time to get a good education.

THE VIDEO CARD

Begin your research with the video card (Figure 4–2), since this choice will dictate the other parameters, right down to the motherboard in your computer. Many video cards are available, with new contenders appearing in the marketplace on a regular basis. The price and output quality of video cards varies a great deal. For full-screen, high-resolution video, suitable for semi-professional use, expect to spend $1,000 or more. Most cards accept standard composite and S-video input and output signals. The better products go to the next level, with a digital (FireWire) interface or with component connections compatible with the broadcast tape format Beta SP.

Real-Time Video Cards

Since its inception, the real drawback to nonlinear editing has been the render time. Virtually all systems today can play digitized video in real time. However, when it comes to even the simplest of special effects, the nonlinear software must do what amounts to the creation of an animation sequence, processing one frame of video at a time, "rendering" the effect before it can be played in real time. *Rendering* means the editing software must mathematically calculate how the video changes from one frame to the next, as images dissolve from one to another or a title sweeps into view. Depending on the speed of your computer's video card, the computer's central processor speed, and the amount of variables in the video image, each frame of video can take from several seconds to over a minute in the rendering process. For a finished effect that plays for several seconds in real time, render time can extend to 30 minutes or more. It is easy to see how rendering can be a bottleneck in the production process.

However that's all beginning to change. Manufacturers have begun to offer hot rod versions of their video cards that take the wait out of render-

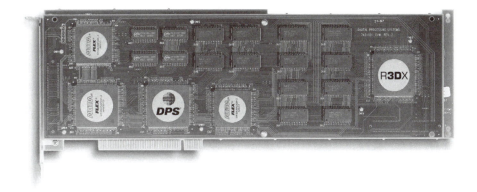

Figure 4–2. The video card. The choice of video card will be the most important decision in setting up an AV system.

ing, delivering video with actual real-time effects. Now you can have the freedom of nonlinear editing but also the speed you left behind with linear editing. Such new developments are making the switch to nonlinear editing more and more attractive to end users.

The system works because, even though fancy 3D effects are the ultimate in eye candy, for most projects the elegant and simple dissolve is the effect of choice. Dissolves are much less demanding on the computer's calculating capabilities than 2D and 3D effects, enabling the real-time video card to perform at maximum efficiency. And the real-time effects option goes beyond basic dissolves. Transition effects such as the push, picture in picture, slides, flips, and a host of other simple wipes can be performed in real time, too, giving the video editor plenty of speedy options.

The performance of the enhanced video card also adds acceleration to effects that, while not processed in real time, can be rendered at a much faster speed. For example, some product literature claims that certain effects contained on Adobe Premier are accelerated by up to 600%.

Look for continual improvements on the horizon. New video cards are being released that promise to take these capabilities to another level, giving you 3D-type effects in real time. Based on the technology currently used by the big boys in broadcast, each new development represents a breakthrough in the cost barrier for desktop video capabilities.

Size and Shape Can Make a Difference

Because they vary in size and shape, the first challenge you may face is fitting the video card into the PCI slot on the computer motherboard and within the confines of your computer housing. Video cards can be fairly large, and the physical layout of your motherboard suddenly is relevant. The Pentium chip, with a heat sink and cooling fan attached above it, often is placed in line with the PCI slots. With the larger video cards this can be an obstruction, making insertion of the card impossible. Beyond this concern, there are requirements for specific BIOS characteristics, so it is prudent to obtain recommendations from the video card manufacturer to ascertain the suitability of your current (or proposed) motherboard.

Still another decision in selecting a video card relates to the format in which you will work. All systems handle composite and most include S-video. Digital FireWire connections are a viable option, found on more and more cards. Serious professionals may want to consider a card with component RGB input and output, used by the Beta SP tape format.

WHAT ABOUT AUDIO?

Let's not forget that audio is an essential part of video editing, and something you also must consider when selecting your system. Some of the more expensive video card options include audio capability, thus ensuring that both the video and audio stay together in perfect sync. To keep down costs, some video card manufacturers require you to have a separate audio card, using another slot inside your computer. This indeed may save you money, since most computer users already have audio cards with their systems. While in general this should work OK, be aware that users in the field complain that sometimes the audio and video can drift apart or lose sync. This manifests itself as the words not quite matching the lips of the person talking on-screen, with either the video or audio running slightly behind. Take a piece of advice: Talk to others already using the system you are considering to learn if they have found this to be a problem. Find these people by surfing video-related Internet chat sites or by getting your local video hardware or software retailer to give you a list of end users in your area. It pays to know what you are getting into. You may find that, by the time you purchase the video card and audio card separately, a single card that does everything may be more cost competitive than it first appeared.

One distinction between low-end and high-end audio cards or video cards with audio capability is the type of audio input connection (Figure 4–3).

Figure 4–3. Audio connectors (from left to right): RCA phono, XLR, 1/4-inch phone.

The typical connection is the RCA phono, a simple push-on connector, which in terms of quality can be compared to composite video. The upgrade from this is the three-pin XLR connector. Here the audio signal is protected from outside interference by an outside, grounded shield. The shield absorbs and deflects audio monsters such as AC hum or reception of unwanted signals like radio stations. In general, the resulting audio is cleaner, and your edited productions more professional. One other connector commonly found on audio gear, like mixing boards and multitrack audio recorders, is the 1/4-inch phono connector. For maximum versatility, keep a collection of audio adapters on hand so you can make any connector work with your system.

FAST AND WIDE VIDEO DRIVES

As mentioned previously, the most expensive part of your system may not be your computer or video card but your hard drives. Video eats up vast amounts of hard drive space, so no matter how much you have, you'll always want more. The drives are accessed with a special controller card, a SCSI (pronounced scuzzy) card, linked via a cable to the motherboard.

Ultrafast and -wide SCSI-controlled hard drives are two to four times the cost of standard drives. A 4-gigabyte hard drive will deliver only up to 20 minutes of storage space. Before you get too optimistic, you should know that a 5-minute edited project probably will use up 15 minutes of hard drive space. Remember that your edited program is derived of selected portions of video clips. In other words, you may digitize or record a 30-second video clip, then later select only a 15-second portion to use in your edited program. However the entire digitized clip remains on your hard drive, taking up space. Of course there will be audio on your drive, too, as well as other things that use up hard drive memory, such as titles, transitions, and special effects. These all add up, and together they fill your drive.

Working in the Windows NT operating system allows you to use the NTFS style formatting on your media drive. NTFS is inherently more cohesive and reliable, since it is not subject to fragmentation, like drives formatted in the more common FAT configuration. However Windows 95 and 98 does not recognize the NTFS format, so if you elect to use both (NT and 95 or 98) operating systems, data saved in NTFS is not available to your Windows 95 or 98 programs. If this is a problem, you simply can format your media drive with the FAT system.

Still another consideration when selecting your media drive is speed. Not all drives are created equal, and a faster drive or drive array will translate into better video resolution. This is because a higher-resolution image contains more information. Your drive's ability to retrieve that data efficiently will enable you to digitize with lower compression ratios, resulting in higher resolution images. Look at rotation speed, typically 4,500 rpm on a nonmedia drive and starting at 5,400 rpm as a minimum for a fast and wide drive. Even better than the fast and wide drives are the Ultrawide drives, with an rpm of 10,000 or more.

The other important number to consider is transfer rate: again the higher number, the better. Compare a standard drive that may have a transfer rate of only 16 megabytes per second with a fast and wide drive's rate of 33 MB/s. Go for an ultra 40 MB/s or more to maximize your capability in all directions.

A fully outfitted video editing system may consist of two or more dedicated video media drives, one or two standard hard drives, as well as other hardware such as a power supply, a CD-ROM drive, a video card, an audio card, a SCSI controller, perhaps even a Zip drive, and a modem. Therefore you may need the larger variety case, called a *full tower,* simply to fit everything inside. These hard drives generate heat and lots of it. You need air circulation to keep things from overheating and two or more internal fans generally are required. Some editors leave the sides off their computers and use a small room fan blowing on all the electronics to keep temperatures down.

GOING TURNKEY

Presently a number of "turnkey" systems are on the market that will save you an enormous amount of time and energy in putting together a nonlinear video editing system. This is particularly advisable if you have limited experience with computer components. If you decide to build or assemble your own system, try to line up someone with more than basic knowledge of how computer software and hardware interrelate. While it is possible to save several thousand dollars in hard costs, setting up the interface for the variety of elements that must work together to create a successful video editing system can be difficult and confusing. Without question, most of the components used in a Windows-based computer editor are relatively new, and accepted standards that ultimately will force compatibility are still being determined. Much of the new software also increasingly demands precise computer hardware specifications as their functions become more sophisticated.

SAVING YOUR WORK

Most editors often find themselves working on several projects at once. Because storage time on multigigabyte drives is limited, it becomes necessary to dump your projects to some other medium to clear the drives and recover your storage space. Today a common storage medium is the computer-based DAT (digital audiotape; Figure 4–4). The computer's bits and

Figure 4–4. DAT backup recorder. The most common storage medium is the computer-based digital audiotape.

bytes are recorded onto these high-capacity tapes. A single tape can hold almost 2 gigabytes of memory. A large project can be spread across several tapes, and transferring the information from the hard drive to DAT tape is a process that can take hours. Unfortunately it can take just as long to load a project from the DAT tapes back into the computer. This time-consuming operation can be one of the greatest drawbacks to nonlinear editing. It is quite common to run tape backup or retrieval during off hours, such as through the middle of the night, using multitape machines to cycle tapes automatically for large volume backup.

Another storage medium coming into vogue is the removable optical drive. These are like interchangeable hard drives that, while more expensive than a DAT system, are faster to work with. They're too expensive to use for long-term storage but allow you have several edit projects going on at once and can be a nice alternative to permanently installed multigigabyte drives.

SAFETY TIPS

True pain is when the electricity goes out in the middle of a 2-hour render and the interruption corrupts your project. Protect yourself from this and other nightmares with a battery backup. Priced at around $150, battery backup systems maintain their charge through their connection to the wall receptacle and automatically switch to battery power inverted to 110 volts AC whenever power fails. Depending on your storage capacity, rather than continue working, your best option usually is to shut down all systems in a proper manner.

Probably the biggest threat to your system is a power surge, caused by a lightning strike or the rush of power when it returns after a power outage. Your computer and all of its related components should be plugged into a surge protector, often in the form of an AC power strip. Never foolproof, they offer some measure of protection.

The absolute best protection you can give yourself is to unplug all components from power when they are not in use. This end-of-the-day procedure also includes disconnecting the phone line running to your modem, which can be another open door for a power surge caused by a lightning strike. An extra minute a day can save you untold amounts of heartache and frustration later.

There is no easy answer to the question of what system to buy at what price. So much depends on your needs and personal budget. But, once you have taken the plunge, you'll find there's no turning back. Nonlinear editing is the truly creative approach for developing a video program, blowing tape-to-tape linear editing straight out of the water. However, when you find yourself faced with unexplained (and exasperating) crashes that dump you so unceremoniously from your treasured video project that has a deadline of tomorrow morning, you will find really one rule must be remembered when dealing in this tenuous, temperamental world of electronic media: *Save your work.*

The Home Video Editing Challenge

5

Nonlinear editing—a magic world where tape no longer exists, where editing is free and easy. Indeed nonlinear editing can be like a dream come true, existing in many shapes and forms. It gives the video editor a freedom to create that linear editing never can come close to. Let's take a look at just exactly what nonlinear editing is and what it can do.

LINEAR VERSUS NONLINEAR EDITING

Editing is the task of taking selected scenes from one or more prerecorded videotapes and assembling those scenes in a specific order to create a completed program, be it a vacation video, broadcast TV show, wedding, or industrial marketing video. With *linear* (tape-to-tape) *editing*, video from source tapes, your original material, is recorded to an edited master tape. If your editing gear will perform "insert" edits, it is possible to do things like record the video separately from the audio tracks or place new video over old at any point on the tape. Once the new video is recorded, the old video is gone forever. Want to change the order of your scenes or add a new scene between what you've done already? With linear editing basically you have to start over, beginning with the new scene and reediting everything after that.

Nonlinear editing is just what the term implies: not in a line. Instead of accessing data on a tape, which requires that you pass points A and B to reach point C, video that is "digitized" onto a hard drive is randomly accessible. This also means that, once acquired, scenes can be manipulated without consideration to what comes either before or after that particular video event. Insertions, multiple layered transitions, effects, and more can be applied at any point during the editing process. This provides enormous flexibility and seemingly limitless options for sculpting your video program.

The beauty of nonlinear editing is the cut and paste timeline (Figure 5–1). Once you have digitized selected scenes from your tapes onto the computer's hard drive, you can arrange these clips according to your script and your liking. Nonlinear editing provides you with the ability to drag and drop, copy, delete, replace, insert, and more, all of which are virtually impossible with linear tape editing.

In some ways nonlinear editing can be compared to writing with a word processor. The timeline is your document and each scene a paragraph. You can rearrange paragraphs, that is, scenes, with simple keystroke and or mouse driven commands. If you insert a new scene, everything moves over to accommodate the change. You can lengthen the timing on a

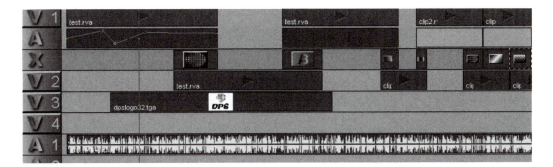

Figure 5–1. Typical nonlinear timeline. The project timeline stands at the heart of the nonlinear approach to video editing.

scene transition such as a dissolve, change the transition from a dissolve to a tumbling cube, add a title—you have the power to experiment indefinitely, complete flexibility with no commitment. This unparalleled sense of freedom is the primary attraction of nonlinear editing.

Nonlinear editing systems are hardware and software combinations, which operate inside a computer. If you already own a suitable computer and video hardware, then your shopping may be limited to selecting the nonlinear editing software that best satisfies your needs.

SELECTING NONLINEAR EDITING SOFTWARE

More than a dozen nonlinear software systems already are available, with new contenders entering the marketplace everyday. With so many nonlinear editing systems arriving on the scene (Figures 5–2 and 5–3), deciding which system is right for you requires a great deal of comparison and study. By their very nature most systems share common elements and functions; however, in the end each takes its own approach to the creation of what is hoped to be an intuitive operation.

The challenge is the same in all cases: collect your video and audio clips and arrange them onto a timeline, complete with effects, transitions, and titles. Just how this is accomplished distinguishes a program that is easy

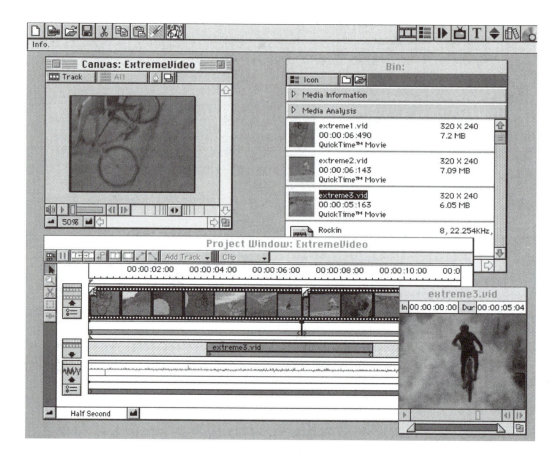

Figure 5–2. Editing screen. Virtually all nonlinear edit systems share common features: a timeline (bottom), a project window (upper left), a media library (upper right), a clip preview window (lower right).

to use from one that requires complicated commands. Of course, with greater versatility comes a necessary increase in complexity and therefore longer learning time.

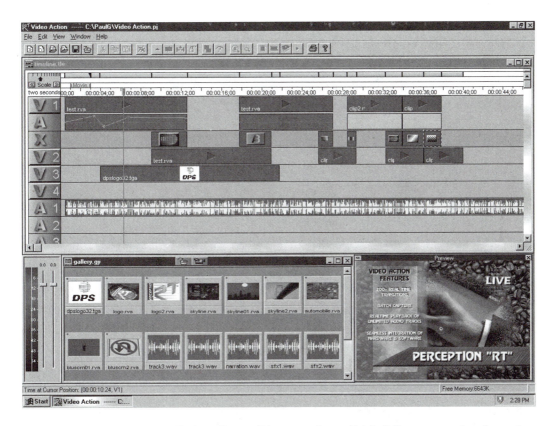

Figure 5–3. A different system. Each nonlinear editing system has a slightly different approach to the way it layers audio, video, transitions, and titles.

BATCH CAPTURE AND VCR CONTROL

The first step in any nonlinear editing project is digitizing the raw material from your videotapes onto the computer. This can be done more or less manually, playing tapes from your camcorder or VCR and instructing the computer when to begin "recording," sending the video and audio signals to the hard drive in their new digital form. Because the source material is coming from a tape, be it S-VHS, Hi8, Betacam, or whatever, many nonlinear systems are designed to act as edit controllers and will interact with most prosumer and industrial VCRs. Controlling the camcorder or VCR from the computer is a distinct advantage, giving you greater control and convenience. It also can make it possible to perform "batch capture" (Figure 5–4). This allows you to go through your source tape, select the In and Out points for all of your scenes, then leave the computer and VCR unattended while they relocate and digitize all your material in the computer. The initial digitization also can be done at a low resolution to save disk space. Later, after you have made all of your editing decisions, the batch capture feature can redigitize only the footage from your tapes necessary for the final high-resolution edit.

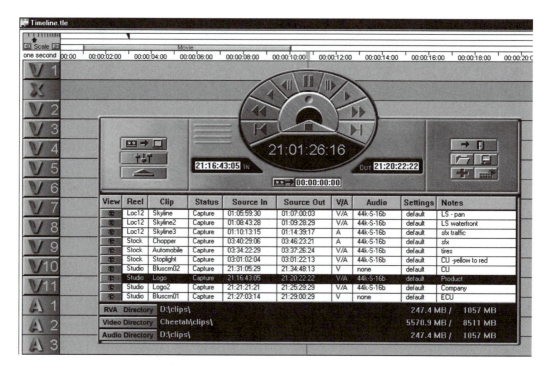

Figure 5–4. Video clip library and batch capture screen. All systems digitize video, but those with batch capture use the computer to do most of the work for you.

COMPRESSION AND RESOLUTION

As discussed earlier, video information requires a lot of space on a hard drive, especially if you want your images to maintain high-quality, full-screen resolution. To get the video onto the hard drive, the nonlinear system uses a compression scheme to squeeze the video signal in size. When the video is recalled from the hard drive, the images are decompressed and returned to their original form or a close approximation. Most systems let you decide the level of compression that will be applied (Table 5–1).

Low-resolution storage requires less memory space and allows you to fit more minutes or hours of video on the hard drive. This can be useful for what's known as *off-line editing*. Off-line editing is used when you are roughing out the form and structure of your finished program. Since this edited version will not be seen by your final audience, resolution is not critical. In addition to greater storage space on the hard drive, processing time from the hard drive is faster. A 100 to 1 compression factor allows you to store as much as an hour and a half of video per gigabyte (GB) of memory. Go to a 3 to 1 compression rate and that same gigabyte will store only a little under 3 minutes of video. It makes sense to start in the low-resolution mode until you have a pretty good idea what scenes will be used in the final edit. You may dump in an hour of video at first, whittling that down to a finished

Table 5–1. Compression Ratios to Hard Disk Storage Time

Digitize Quality Setting (KB per frame)	MB per Minute of Video	Minutes per GB on a Media Drive
60	108	9.3
80	144	6.9
100	180	5.6
120	216	4.6
140	252	4
160	288	3.5

show of perhaps only 5 or 10 minutes. Then you can go back and redigitize the material to be used in the final edit to the hard drive at a much higher resolution.

TRACKS AND LAYERS

A big advantage of nonlinear editing is that, once the material has been dumped inside the computer, you are in a completely digital domain, which means virtually no signal generation loss or degradation. Linear editing commonly requires the video producer to drop down a generation; that is, copy the edited tape to a second tape to add titles or for special transition effects such as an A/B dissolve. Nonlinear editing does all this inside the computer, allowing you to stack various video elements in layers (Figure 5–5). You may experience some loss due to the compression/decompression of the video, but if you use a minimal or even simply a moderate amount of compression, for the most part the loss is negligible, essentially invisible to the untrained eye.

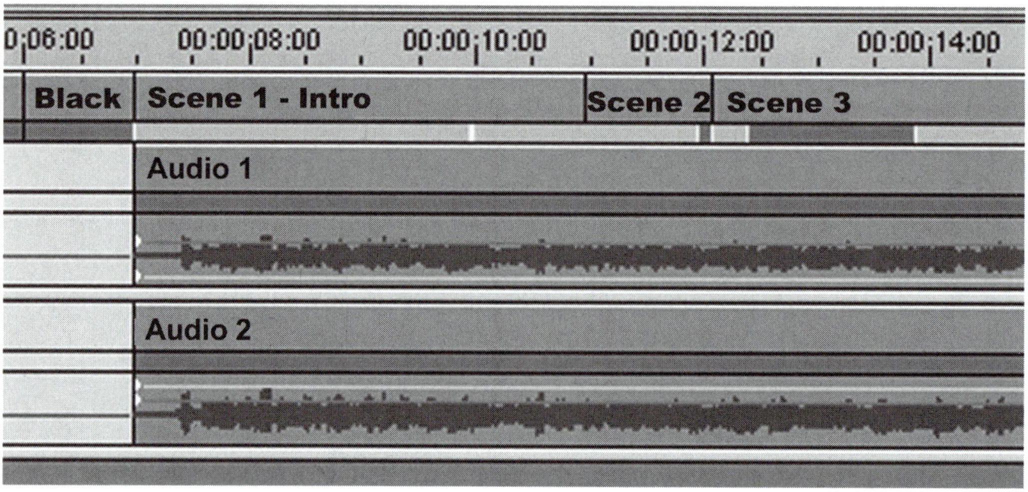

Figure 5–5. A nonlinear editing timeline is composed of many layers of video and audio.

Nonlinear editing programs vary in the number of video and audio layers they provide and in the way the layers or tracks relate to each other. Two tracks of video and four audio tracks are the minimum, although a number of systems give you almost limitless layering. Since a transition essentially is a change from one video scene to another along the timeline, some systems place the two video clips on a single video track with a transition effect linking them together. Additional video tracks could hold the location of titles, picture in picture images, and similar elements. In the end the multiple video layers must be merged into one for final playback of the project.

Because most music is recorded in stereo, virtually all nonlinear editing systems give you at least four audio tracks. The music uses up two tracks (right and left) and that leaves you one track for the natural or background sound associated with your video clip and another for a narrator's voice or any other source of sound such as sound effects.

THE CHARACTER GENERATOR

The titler, or character generator (Figure 5–6), is an integral component of any nonlinear editing software, and most nonlinear editing programs include some sort of character generator as part of the package. This allows you to type away, selecting a font, color, plus expected extras like drop shadows. Titles can be placed over live video or merged with a background screen. Many titlers allow you to import outside elements, such as a logo, and incorporate it with the rest of the title layout.

When it comes to creating titles, font selection (Figure 5–7) is paramount. The better titlers will draw from your computer's collection of True Type and Type 1 fonts. New fonts can be acquired or purchased from a variety of sources, expanding your titling capabilities and variety. However, keep in mind that having too many fonts stored on your hard drive uses up memory, so don't go overboard. Add only the ones you use regularly and a few more that may have specific applications. Leave the rest on the source CD-ROM, accessing them only when you need a fresh look for a title.

The tools that manipulate your fonts and titles separate one system's capabilities from another. Most give you drop shadows (Figure 5–8) and outlines around letters, plus nice things like two-toned gradient fill for the letter face. A high-quality character generator produces antialiased letters and utilizes 32-bit processing, with 24-bit color plus an 8-bit alpha channel, used for superimposing your titles over live video. The 24-bit antialiasing produces letter edges that are clean and smooth, with very little annoying flicker and dot crawl, common to lower-quality titlers.

SPECIAL EFFECTS AND TRANSITIONS

When comparing nonlinear software, there is always the question of special effects and transitions. The basic dissolve is a given. Often a variety of basic wipes (Figure 5–9A), zooms, pushes, and squeezes are available. Page turns (Figure 5–9B) are very popular and carry a statement about the quality of the effects. A page turn can be very plain, with little texture or depth, or deluxe, with live, moving video on both sides of the page and a shadow that

Figure 5–6. Character generator screen. Professional looking titles (character generation) are one of the computer's strongest contributions to video editing.

can be adjusted for density, angle, and length, plus a sheen or reflection on the back side of the page, which adds more realism to the effect.

Filter effects allow you to add texture like a mask over your video images for a different look. These range from the traditional posterization to options like blur, color processing for hue and saturation control, brightness, and contrast.

The picture in picture (PIP, Figure 5–10) effect places a video image from another layer over the primary video track, just as it would a title. The

Figure 5–7. Font samples. A good font selection brings variety and style to your titles.

superimposed video or PIP can zoom from barely visible to any size, while moving across the screen.

CHROMINANCE AND LUMINANCE KEYING

Another important feature to compare is chrominance and luminance keying. This is another method for layering or superimposing one video track over another. A chroma key (Figure 5–11) is based on color and typically works like this. A subject is videotaped against a solid color background, usually blue or green but it can be most any color. The computer allows you

Figure 5–8. Drop shadows, outlines, and other effects not only look good, they help accent your titles and make them easier to read.

to fill the solid color area behind the subject with another, selected background, be it a video clip, a texture, or an imported graphic. The subject then is superimposed over this new background. Achieving good results requires careful lighting of the subject and chroma key background when recording on tape; however, the quality of the chroma key software also has a direct effect on the final image. Poor chroma key systems can leave a raggedy color halo or trailing edge around the subject. Some systems will perform the key or transparent cutout based on a range of hues rather than a single color, extending the latitude and variance in shading caused by uneven lighting.

A.

Figure 5–9. Transitions (see color insert) help keep the viewer interested and allow the video production to flow smoothly from one scene to the next: (A) basic dissolve; (B) page turn.

B.

Figure 5–9. (continued).

Luminance keying performs a similar function; however, the keying process is based on shades of light and dark rather than color. Titlers or character generators typically use a sort of luminance keying to superimpose titles, placing the title graphics onto solid black backgrounds that appear transparent when placed over video. Chroma keying generally is preferred when using live subjects, because luminance keying is likely to cause shadows and dark areas of the video image to become transparent along with the background.

Figure 5–10. PIP (picture in picture) is an effect that layers a small representation of one video clip over another (see color insert).

DONGLES

More and more software companies are ensuring against unauthorized use of their program through the use of a dongle (Figure 5–12), and your nonlinear editing system is no exception. A dongle is a minicircuit housed inside a multipin connector that must be plugged into your computer's parallel port before the program will function. Without the dongle the program is disabled, but when in place, the proprietary code inside the dongle opens the door to all the goodies. Companies also use dongles to facilitate program upgrades. As the software is further developed and owner–users

Figure 5–11. Chroma key before and after images (see color insert). The color blue is passed through the chroma keyer and made transparent. The chroma keyed image appears superimposed over the new background video.

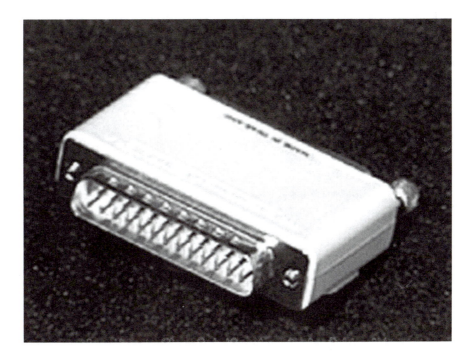

Figure 5–12. Dongles, like this one, protect the software developer from unauthorized use of its programs. When a program uses this form of protection, the dongle must be connected to the end user's computer parallel port before the software will function.

are offered added features, new dongles are part of the package. What if your parallel port already has a dongle? No problem. Most dongles are made to be passive, allowing you to stack one after the other so that each program sees what it needs to operate. It is not uncommon to have four or more dongles stacked one after the other, each required for different software. Signals to your printer will not be hindered by the dongle circuitry, so cables can be placed at the end of the chain.

ADDING MORE SPECIAL EFFECTS THROUGH PLUG-INS

Are you interested in some serious eye candy for your computer video workstation? Most people are, and these days it has become a necessary part of your editing arsenal. Let's face it, you just aren't sitting on the cutting edge without the ability to create flashy effects and transitions. Most nonlinear editing programs come with a limited number of built-in wipes and effects, which can be enhanced through additional, optional software, either from the parent company or from third party manufacturers. The term *plug-in* means that the outside software integrates directly into the editing program. Call up the Effects window in your nonlinear editor and the plug-in features are available, ready to be accessed. Since not all programs work together, most special effects programs also function as stand-alones, with the ability to import and export video and audio files directly.

However, the faster your processor, the more you'll find yourself using your computer for special effects. Rendering complex effects always takes time, but what comes out the other side makes it seem well worth the wait.

Fortunately the special effects programs keep improving, and each new release is better optimized to take advantage of the faster processing speeds found on current computers. You'll find rendering to be up to 50% faster, resulting in greater productivity and efficiency.

Most special effects programs include a great many prepackaged transitions as well as custom tools for an infinite variety of options. You may find customizing to be difficult at first, but with a little patience they allow you to dive in deeper, developing your own interpretation of more common effects.

The difference between 2D and 3D effects obviously is dimension. But what gives a 3D-image depth? Light. Light creates shadow and illustrates form. Effects programs help you establish dimension by giving you access to digital sources of light. Turn a light source off or on. Vary the light intensity from a soft ambient glow to a stronger but still diffused light or add a bright beam for a specular highlight. You also often can control a light's position and distance.

A variation on the special effects option is the use of filters (Figure 5–13). Behaving almost like a new layer of video, filters can perform important functions like color correction or can change your video's appearance like shooting through a tinted lens. Other filters modify the

Figure 5–13. Filter effects, like ripple and bulge, can modify the digitized video in a wide variety of ways (see color insert).

video, adding a ripple, bulge, or wave, distorting the video while mapping it to a predetermined form. You can transform your video in ways you never imagined.

CREATING DIGITAL TITLE SCREENS

In the real world of editing, the computer and its assorted software programs have become essential, not just as tapeless nonlinear editing systems but as important illustrators and title machines. In fact, the computer's first link with video nearly a decade ago was as a cost-effective titler. Simple 8-bit software combined with hardware add-ons permitted end users to overlay graphics on top of video. Clearly, this was just the beginning.

PAINTING AND DRAWING SOFTWARE

Every editor needs at least one painting or drawing program, and the software created for desktop publishing interact perfectly with desktop video. The current standard is 32-bit software, promising higher-resolution images with better tools for creating custom title screens and more. Choosing the right software for your system becomes an important decision: It will cost you some bucks and it is a decision that you will live with for years to come.

Why do you need an art program? Because it's the perfect way to create quick background screens, and even titles. A frozen image captured from video may need to be improved. In the hands of a skilled artist, a drab storefront can be made to shine. The talented computer artist can do anything, from erasing graffiti to replacing telephone poles and wires with a beautiful blue sky. A black-and-white logo from a newspaper can be turned into color, getting rid of all the ad copy and other irrelevant material. Backdrops are built out of unrelated objects and settings, combining elements from different shots and locations into eye-catching art.

Tools of the Trade

Many of the art programs used in video production have been a part of the print graphics toolkit for many years. Consequently the software purchased today is the result of many generations of program evolution. Other programs are relatively new or perhaps brand new for use in video editing. All reflect the growing influence of desktop video, with more and more features that apply specifically to video production.

Unlike paint programs, which are based on pixels, drawing or vector programs use objects defined by lines and points that can be scaled to any size while maintaining their resolution and proportion. It is important to make the distinction between vector-based (Figure 5–14), or drawing, programs and pixel-based, or raster (painting), programs. In math, a vector is a line. It can be straight or curved and, in its own way, is a very linear approach to drawing or creating objects. Technically a vector program is a drawing tool. Unlike a painting program, it has the ability to expand or reduce image size mathematically with no change in resolution. Vector programs give you the ability to enter text along any path, straight or curved, then edit it with a multitude of tools. You can add thickness, shadows, or outlines or make text 3D, blend colors, create transparent type outlines, rotate text, wrap letters around objects, and much more.

One could say the pixel-based (Figure 5–15), painting, program deals more with appearance. Antialiasing in pixel-based programs blends a range of colors to make edges appear smoother and curves more natural. They eliminate jagged stairstep lines or hard color divisions, which can cause annoying dot crawl on TV images. A complete video production kit should have both types of programs, each used for different applications or for different stages of a project. Keep in mind, however, that since your screen is made up of a grid of pixels, all products ultimately render your image into pixels for display.

No matter what program you choose, there is a huge learning curve when you first get started, as you learn about the tools and features and how to make them do what you want. Fortunately, virtually all art programs share similar functions, tools, and symbols (Figure 5–16). For example, an icon of a spilling bucket of paint usually symbolizes a fill tool, used to fill selected areas with a new color. Other common tools include a paintbrush, a pencil, and box and circle tools, to name a few. You can vary the size and width of your paint stroke or pencil line or use an airbrush to spray color. The mouse or electronic sketchpad and on-screen cursor direct your interface with the screen image.

Because the majority of the work done with art programs is for the print industry, many contain a great degree of sophistication unnecessary for video work. This can make them confusing at times. Again, it will just take a while as you learn how to navigate the program and determine which tools and commands are appropriate for video and which are not.

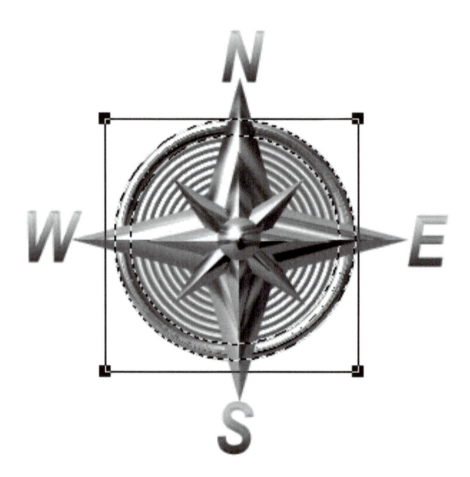

Figure 5–14. A vector-based drawing program can expand or reduce its image size mathematically with no change in resolution.

Importing Images and Backgrounds

The first trick is to get the image, logo, or background into your computer. The images you work with come from everywhere. They could include a photo or a logo on stationery, business cards, or larger forms such as outdoor signs and billboards. One tool for capturing these images is right in your hands: your camcorder. When on location, be on the lookout for anything that can be used later for a title screen. It might be a storefront, a

Figure 5–15. Extreme closeup of a bitmap showing pixelation. Painting programs are pixel based, functioning as bitmaps, which identify the location and color of every bit present of the screen.

table setting in a restaurant, or even a T-shirt with the company logo. It's better to take letterhead and printed material back to the studio where you have better control over lighting. Another tool for importing images into your editing system is a scanner, which can give you even higher resolution than your camcorder.

Fortunately nonlinear editing software sets you up perfectly for importing images into an art program. Because you primarily are creating title screens and backgrounds, nonmoving images, all you really need is one frame of video. This frame must be converted into a form accepted by your art software. You can choose from several different file formats, such as .tiff, bitmaps, and .jpeg, all basically digital renditions of a single-frame image. When capturing an image from your camcorder, depending

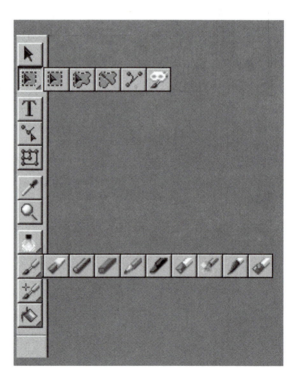

Figure 5–16. This art program tool bar shows that virtually all art programs use similar functions, tools, and symbols.

on your system's capabilities, you may be able to make it function as a frame grabber or it may be necessary to first digitize the video into your computer.

From there you can "export" a single video frame as a graphic file to your hard drive, which then can be imported into your art program. You modify the image in the art program through painting, coloring, enhancing, erasing, and cropping—whatever you may need to do. Once the modified image is saved, the file can be imported back into your editing project. Place the frame on your timeline as a background or as the title screen itself. It can be stored on your hard drive just like any other video clip and used over and over again within a project or in any future projects.

Desktop Publishing Meets Desktop Video

As just mentioned, the perfect tool for bringing photos, logos, and printed images into your art program is a scanner. Even with the best camcorder, you will still get a sharper copy of a logo or other flat images using a color scanner. The advantage here is that the scanned image is instantly digital, with no other conversion necessary. Image resolution is variable, depending on the requirements of the project or the complexity of the image. Once scanned, save the image in whatever format is appropriate, usually a bitmap or .tiff, .jpeg, or .gif file. Art programs are designed to work in conjunction with a scanner, and in fact, many scanners come with an art program as part of their package.

One secret in the publishing world over the years has been clip art and other copyright-free textures and backgrounds. This element now comes to video in the form of CD-ROM images. Why spend hours creating a striking background when you can have an incredibly beautiful image at your fingertips in seconds? So much is there to choose from: glorious sunsets, wood grains, marble and granite, seascapes, and other generic backdrops. Some collections are a bit expensive, while others are very, very affordable. They become part of your kit, pulled out of the hat like a magician's rabbit, to amaze your clients or simply to add class to your personal videos.

Painting and Special Effects

As video becomes established as a digital medium, developers are releasing painting programs specifically designed for video production. The video-specific art software can be used to assemble 2D and 3D animated effects, as well as create filter layers that permit the editor to modify or enhance a video segment without affecting the original material. Indeed, the same software available to you is used daily in broadcast television, creating multilayered images or natural effects like realistic lightning and fire. You can have a blue lightning bolt streak through the sky, strike a person walking down the road, and explode the person into tiny particles. It's nothing short of amazing.

Art programs that incorporate elements of animation allow you to paint or work over a timeline and not just on a single-frame image. This lets you to perform tasks such as rotoscoping, a popular effect that combines animation with real images, often seen in music videos where the performer is outlined in a Day-Glo color.

So, How Do You Choose?

As usual, your choice of an art or animation program depends on your requirements. Your goal is to produce visual excitement that will hold a viewer's attention and tell the story effectively. Art and animation programs are indispensable for the design, creation, and enhancement of your video material, and merit your serious attention as you build your video workstation.

COMPUTER MONITORS VERSUS NTSC TELEVISION

Novice editors are often disappointed to discover that the beautiful images they create on their computer screen often are much different when reproduced on an NTSC television. There are several reasons for this. Computer monitors are capable of displaying many more color variations and shades, up to 16 million colors on an optimized computer system, compared to approximately 32,000 with NTSC. Colors will not be as intense in NTSC and the computer even can generate colors that are considered "illegal" to broadcast. Oversaturated reds can bleed out of their edges, whiter whites can send your TV screen into distortion. Some art programs can compensate for this and will help you avoid problems by ensuring that your colors are video safe. For best results, always monitor your work on a computer screen and an NTSC television simultaneously.

PUTTING IT ALL TOGETHER

Start out with an initial nonlinear program, then enhance your capabilities with plug-in effects and other outside software. The home video editing challenge can take many forms and will extend as far as you wish to take it. Whether your goal is a simple home video or a full-blown show for television, the basic computer with affordable hardware and software puts it all within reach.

Unlimited Audio for Video

6

Too often audio becomes the forgotten element in video work, although no professional would discount its importance. Even the very best video images will not overcome poor audio quality in video programs. At the very least, a good audio track is supposed to be seamless with the visuals, and the viewer should not even notice it as a separate element. At best, superior audio can add enormously to the impact of the visuals—just turn down the sound in your next video rental and notice how frightened, moved, or excited you become without sound to drive the experience.

Just as video has become another mass of bits and bytes in the computer age, so too has audio. Editing directly on your PC has many advantages, not the least of which is the maintenance of crystal clear quality throughout the process. Add to that the convenience of manipulating audio along with visual information, cut and paste features, instantaneous previews, and unparalleled timing accuracy—and you have a strong case for the use of computer software for audio recording and sound enhancement.

Sound is an integral component to any video production, from the live sound that takes place when recording an event to sound that is added later, such as narration, music, or sound effects. During the editing process, the ability to layer or mix sound requires certain tools that can make the videographer's job easier—or for that matter possible. You can take a number of routes to arrive at the destination: enhanced or "sweetened" sound that gives your video production depth, dynamics, mood, and better entertainment value.

The majority of video editing software provides little, if any, capability to modify audio. Other than volume and pan adjustments, your audio tracks must be ready to go once they are on the nonlinear editing timeline.

As in video editing, software is available that gives you total control over audio files (Figure 6–1). These tools enhance your creativity or simply allow you to adjust the audio to better suit your needs.

Audio software can be divided into two camps: multitrack recording and audio processing. The computer's digital multitrack recording capability allows you to create at home multilayered audio performances that once were the sole domain of professional studios. Audio processors add effects, compression, extension, distortion, and all manner of exotic enhancements.

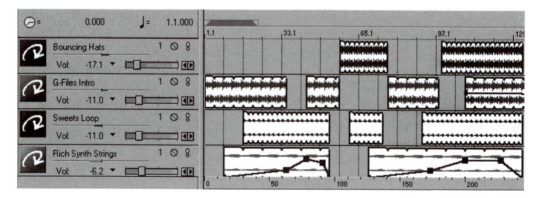

Figure 6–1. Sonic Foundry's software packages let you manipulate your sound in a variety of ways: stretch, compress, and edit your audio as well as add effects like reverberation.

The standard format for audio is the .wav file. A .wav file is simply a digital format specifically configured for audio, just as bitmap or .jpeg is a format for graphic images. The sound quality ranges from adequate to excellent, depending on the quality of the original recording and the bandwidth of the processed file, anything from the limited frequency range of a phone line to the full spectrum of a music CD. Sound files can be either 8 or 16 bit, and sampling rates can range from 2,000 to 60,000 Hz.

Audio editing and recording is a remarkably straightforward process, with visual windows giving you indications of level control and other information regarding your activities. Editing sound files is not unlike working with a video editor. You work with a visual timeline, then cut, copy, paste, overwrite, trim, preview, and more—all these are available with standard Windows icons. There is also a great variety of detailed sound-shaping tools, such as chorus, delay, distortion, pitch, flange/wah-wah, reverberation, and vibrato. In fact, it's a bit of a challenge to think of something that you can't do to a piece of audio.

THE SOUND OF MUSIC

Music plays an especially important role in video, and the music video has become a genre unto itself. Music can set the mood, by adding excitement, sentiment, or even humor. Its other role is to provide unity, giving the video a cohesive feeling, tying everything together.

Once you decide you need music, where do you get it? Well most editors buy it. Although people commonly add their favorite songs to home video productions, it is illegal to use copyrighted music in a commercial production unless permission is obtained and royalties are paid. Even a home video could cross the line into the gray area of copyright infringement if it is entered in a national contest or placed on public display. In response to the need for affordable music, buy-out (copyright-free) music CD libraries (Figure 6–2) have become available at reasonable prices, following on the coattails of the desktop video revolution. Another source for stock music and sounds are digital libraries prepared especially for the computer. These .wav files can be imported directly into your system.

Confused about what you need and where to start? As always, a lot must be learned, but fortunately, with a little basic knowledge it really is not

Figure 6–2. Every video editor needs a collection of copyright-free music.

that complicated. The real question is, "How do you get the sound into your computer and what can you do with it once it's there?"

VIDEO FOLLOWS AUDIO

The computer has become a powerful audio tool, giving the videographer expanded digital capabilities that years ago were unavailable or unaffordable. For example, most industrial video editing VCRs are limited to only two audio tracks, stereo channels right and left. However, a video production can require several audio tracks: one for the natural sound, another for a narrator's voice, and two more for music. Most nonlinear computer-based editing systems give you four or more audio tracks to work with.

Many editors begin their work on a production by first creating the audio tracks. The video then is inserted to follow or correspond to the audio. For example, the narrator describes or talks about what is taking place on the screen. The pace of his or her speaking defines the timing, which the video must follow. By creating the audio mix first you ensure that all audio levels are properly balanced. Music volume is adjusted so that it does not overpower or cover up the voice of the narrator or the natural sound of the scene.

HARDWARE REQUIREMENTS

To work with sound on a computer, you need a sound card. Many different ones are available and in a range of prices, depending on their fidelity and capabilities. Some video cards for nonlinear editing include audio circuitry in their makeup. This can be important, since quite often the video and sound are closely related, such as when a person speaks on-camera. Of course we expect the voice and video to match perfectly. However when the audio card and video card are separate, sometimes it is possible for the video and audio to drift apart, become "out of sync." Even a difference of a few frames, fractions of a second, can cause the video and audio to be out of kilter, with the result quite unsettling. The problem can be subtle or in extreme cases plainly obvious. The mismatch results from the two cards separately receiving their timing information from the computer's internal clock. When both audio and video are processed on the same card, they share timing from the same clock source, ensuring perfect synchrony. Combination video and audio cards tend to be a bit more expensive, designed specifically for nonlinear editing. However, in the end they can be well worth the extra investment.

It is up to you to determine which type of audio card will suit your needs and pocketbook. The output of your sound card will send audio signals to speakers built into the computer or external speakers powered by their own amplifier. For computerized digital (nonlinear) editing, the sound card is what drives your audio, be it voice, music, or sound in general. Eventually the sound will leave the computer and enter a recording deck, Audio Out from the computer sound card, Audio In on the VCR.

MORE MUSIC

The video editor always is on the lookout for new sources of copyright-free music to back up productions. Ideally the producer has music custom created that matches the tone and mood of the video, as well as its length. Music that comes to a definite conclusion in time with the video adds finesse and a professional touch. Fortunately software tools for your computer (Figure 6–3) make it possible to create great sounding music, whether you're a tone-deaf amateur or a serious musician.

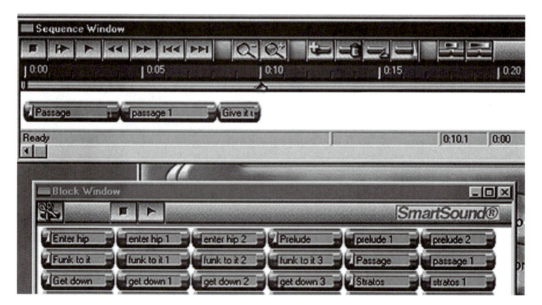

Figure 6–3. Sonic Desktop lets you create custom music by making a series of choices, such as application, and length.

STRIKE UP THE BAND

Ever wish you could be in a band? Most of us have at one time or another, but the logistics of assembling a group of cohesive musicians into a musical ensemble is never an easy task, not to mention the talent that you must possess. If you have an urge to express yourself but could use just a little help, a variety of computer driven options (Figure 6–4) make it easy for you to put together your own music, create original songs and compositions with a minimal amount of musical background or knowledge.

While you don't need to know how to read music or even keep a beat, some programs require you to have an understanding of basic chord progressions and what notes or keys work together. It essentially works like this. First you enter in the chord pattern using whole note names, like A, D, and E.

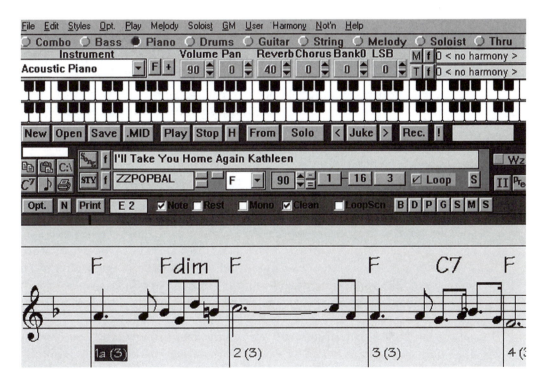

Figure 6–4. Band-in-a-Box uses your computer to play every instrument in a band, including drums, bass, keyboard, and guitar.

Then you select a style, and there are dozens to chose from, with several variations on each—rock, country, blues, reggae, jazz—and each has its own interpretation and theme. Play back your composition, and drums, bass, keyboard, guitar, and more are added automatically. It's a great way to sample melodies and put together songs. Speed up or slow down the song at the click of a mouse. Change keys, styles, add or delete—it's all up to you. With a little practice, you'll be cranking out tunes in no time at all.

Often the lead instrument defines the sound of a particular artist or group. Today's software can mimic the styles of famous musicians, giving your music the flair and feel of yesterday or today's most popular performers. It's the perfect trick to give your video production a soundtrack that sounds like a current hit, without crossing over the line of copyright infringement.

GOING TO THE NEXT LEVEL—MIDI

To go further, you have to start learning about another computer audio language, MIDI (music information digital interface). MIDI is digital information that drives specific software to create sounds. It was developed in the 1980s and became an accepted industry standard. Unlike .wav audio files, which can create sound on their own through a sound card, MIDI files must be processed through a sound program and then the sound card. The sound card functions as a D/A (digital to analog) converter to produce the standard audio output signals heard from your speakers.

One advantage of MIDI is that the files are very small and take up little room on a hard drive. They are a way to manipulate high volumes of sound data with very small files. For example, a MIDI file can be placed on a website as a small bit of data. It then uses the computer of the person who is visiting the site to generate the sound, be it music or sound effects. The music will sound somewhat electronic, kind of like a video game, since the programming software that creates full rich instrument sounds simply is not present.

Typically musicians who are serious about songwriting and composition use a computer and a keyboard to generate MIDI files. This is not your regular computer keyboard but a musical instrument keyboard. You know what I mean, electric pianos and organs, instruments that create their sounds electronically, generate tones that mimic traditional instruments or tones that, well, are synthetic.

Describing the MIDI process in basic terms, as the musician plays notes on his or her instrument, an electronic signal is sent to the computer through an audio sound card equipped with MIDI Inputs and Outputs (Figure 6–5). Not all, in fact, most audio cards are not MIDI-compatible. In addition to RCA phono-type connectors, the card must accept special MIDI connectors as shown in Figure 6–6. The computer (with its MIDI-compatible software open) records the data, which can be saved and stored

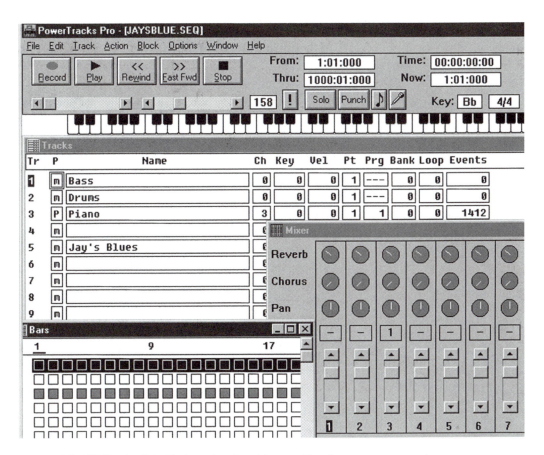

Figure 6–5. MIDI is the digital information that drives specific software to create sounds.

Figure 6–6. To be MIDI-compatible, your audio card must accept these special connectors.

into memory. To play back the MIDI file, the computer program sends a MIDI output signal through the audio card back to the synthesizer keyboard. The synthesizer processes the MIDI signal and, functioning as the digital to analog converter, turns it into sounds that are the same as if the musician were fingering keys and playing live. To hear the music the sounds must leave the keyboard as Audio Out signals, routed either to a set of headphones or an amplifier and speakers. Another possibility is that the audio is sent to the Audio Input of a VCR for recording or audiocassette recorder.

However, there are other ways to work with or get MIDI files. You can purchase music programs with full libraries of MIDI sounds ready for you to use. They might be full songs, individual instruments, or sound effects.

THE NEXT SEQUENCE

If you've ever yearned to exercise a musical creative urge, your computer is an open road, one that will take you as far as you want to go, from the first basic beats to full orchestras. For a relatively minimal investment you can have a true multitrack digital recording studio right in your own home. Whether you just like to play around or consider yourself a serious artist, the digital domain unleashes numerous possibilities. Discover your own creative urges while composing copyright-free music for your videos. Truly, the audio possibilities are virtually unlimited.

Creating Your Own CD-ROM

7

Nothing spells multimedia like CD-ROM. CD-ROMs and their cousin the audio CD have become well established as a format for delivering video and audio information, entertainment, and a whole lot more. Once a mysterious world of programmers and major media developers, today CD-ROM production is within reach of anyone who owns a computer, the right software, and the appropriate hardware. Indeed, your camcorder is an integral part of the equation as a source for images and digital movies. Computer desktop video comes alive in the world of CD-ROM, bringing together your use of art and paint programs, digital audio sources, and nonlinear editing tools into an integrated package.

CD-ROM production is a whole new realm to explore. You can start out with the computer equivalent of training wheels or dive deep into a whole new language, reminiscent of the early BASIC used by computer programmers of the 1980s. Even at it's easiest, there is much to learn and guidelines to follow that will ensure your success. It's entirely within reach, so follow along as we explore creating your own CD-ROM.

THE RIGHT STUFF

One of the best ways to get started is by looking at some finished products, CD-ROMs that have been professionally produced. You'll find that the typical information style CD-ROM (as opposed to a game) begins with an opening "movie" lasting about 30 seconds or so, which then leads you to a menu screen. From the menu screen the user makes choices that lead him or her down various paths to more images and information.

Creating a CD-ROM is essentially a matter of assembling your screens and linking them together in a variety of ways. Begin by developing a structure, the skeleton or bones of the CD-ROM project. Draw your project out on paper, using a block diagram (Figure 7–1) of icons that represent the

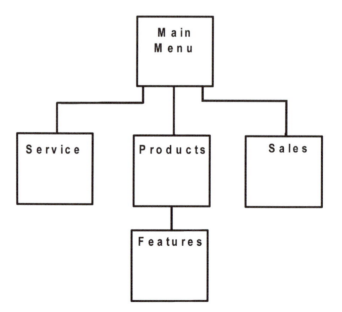

Figure 7–1. Block diagram for a CD-ROM project. Planning your CD-ROM's structure and layout will help facilitate its creation.

various screens linked by lines that form the paths to be followed. Your CD-ROM also could be shown as a timeline with events that take place along the way, in some ways similar to the timeline used in the typical video nonlinear editing scenario. In a way the CD-ROM is like an edited video: Your various screens, animation, and .avi or quick-time videos appear as different scenes in a production. The script you write determines the plot or the path to be followed. Interactivity provides the viewer branches that go off in different directions. The viewer's interest or reaction to on-screen options determines what branches he or she will follow.

It's all simply a matter of assembling a storyboard and fleshing out your project. As in video editing, your CD-ROM tells a story or provides information, using images and sounds in a specified sequence. By taking a little time to plan your project, you'll know what to do next.

ACQUIRING IMAGES

As already discussed, you can import still images, .avi, or digital video movies and computer-generated animation to use in your CD-ROM. These can be things you have created or acquired from the many sources of copyright-free material sold on CD-ROM's, libraries specifically designed for use in multimedia. You'll find these collections to be a great source for generic backgrounds, and simple animation. Usually they are compiled with a common theme, backgrounds, and animation that relate to specific holidays or events or perhaps to business and marketing. CD-ROM libraries also can be a source for a wide range of audio sounds, perfect for making a button go "boink" when you click on it with your mouse.

KNOW YOUR LIMITS

When creating your own source material, you need to know some things to make your project and even the operation of the software run quickly and smoothly. The CD-ROM basically is a digital storage medium, with around 650 megabytes (MB) of storage space. The typical full-screen image created in a paint program can be huge, requiring as much as a 1 MB or more. That is little in relation to the space available on your CD-ROM, but the retrieval time for such a large image can be considerable, making your system work hard and slow.

On a CD-ROM you want the end users to be able to change from screen to screen quickly, so that it holds their attention. Those who must wait a minute or so for a new image to download every time they change screens will get bored in a hurry. For this reason it's best to keep your screen elements at under 500 KB. You do this in a variety of ways. One method is to reduce the size of your image. A look at other CD-ROMs will show you that, other than the background screen, which itself may only use half to two-thirds of your full screen, the screen elements usually are kept small, appearing as little windows and never at full-screen size.

Another way to reduce the digital storage space needed is to reduce the color palette. High-resolution art programs processing 24-bit images work with palettes of 16 million colors. Computer VGA displays work with a palette of only 256 colors, VGA systems use only 16 colors. Knowing this ahead of time, you can design your images to work on anyone's computer and reduce your file size at the same time.

THE DIGITAL ARTIST

Of course the look of your CD-ROM weighs very heavily on your skills as a digital artist, and like any artist, having the right tools at your disposal makes all the difference. Each art, painting, or drawing program has its own strengths; no single piece of software does everything. Most graphic artists like to have a bevy of tools at their disposal. Adding software plug-ins can add tremendously to your capabilities.

A common look in CD-ROMs are buttons with beveled edges. Import your image as a .tiff or bitmap, then turn it into a custom button by beveling the edges and adding a drop shadow, both accomplished easily and automatically as a feature in a number of different programs. Bevels can be "inner" or "outer," round or flat for a variety of different looks. By designing a button with two different styles (for example, embossed for out and recessed for in), you can use one look for the button's standard appearance and have the other appear when it is clicked on by a mouse. Before and after states (Figure 7–2) for your buttons are simple to program into your CD-ROM and make it feel more interactive.

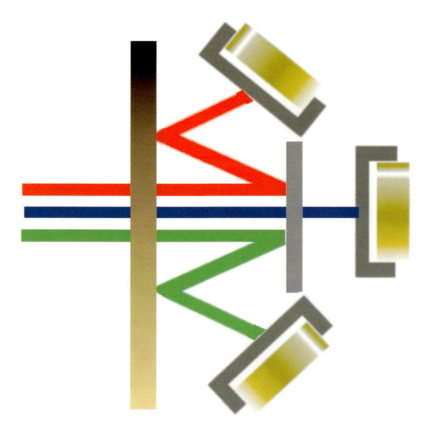

Figure 2–2.   Three-chip configuration. Most camcorders use a single CCD after the camcorder lens to process the video signal. A three-chip system provides more accurate color by dividing the color signal into three components: red, green, and blue (RGB).

Figure 5–9. Transitions help keep the viewer interested and allow the video production to flow smoothly from one scene to the next: (A) basic wipe; (B) page turn.

Figure 5–10.   PIP (picture in picture) is an effect that layers a small representation of one video clip over another.

Figure 5–11. Chroma key before and after images. The color blue is passed through the chroma keyer and made transparent. The chroma-keyed image appears superimposed over the new background video.

Figure 5–13.   Filter effects, like ripple and bulge, can modify the digitized video in a wide variety of ways.

Figure 5–13 (continued).

Figure 9–3.   Examples of background texture.

Figure 9–4. The .gif image file format has a restricted color palette of only 256 colors and is best suited to flat logos and cartoon images.

Figure A–5. Video SpiceRack uses gradient matte overlays to create an infinite variety of transitions.

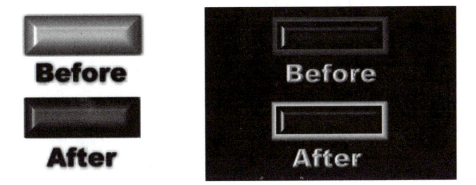

Figure 7–2. Before and after states for your buttons will make your CD-ROM feel more interactive.

BURNING YOUR CD-ROM

To make your CD-ROM, you'll need a dedicated piece of hardware, a CD-ROM recorder (Figure 7–3). This can be an external device or something that fits inside your computer, just like a standard CD-ROM drive. In fact your CD-ROM "burner" also operates as a CD-ROM player. In the last few years prices on recorders have dropped dramatically, from several thousand to now under $500. There are several to choose from, from big name companies like Hewitt Packard and Phillips to newer independents. Check to see the speed of the writer; for example, a four-speed writer needs less time to write the information from your computer to the CD-ROM than a one-speed device.

The price of blank CDs also is much more reasonable, well under $5 apiece. You can record on each CD only one time, so you won't be using them frivolously; but they are affordable and, for the amount of storage space they provide, really pretty economical.

Rewritable CDs are available at about double the cost of the single-use CD-ROMs. They require a special recorder as well, and it remains to be seen whether they will be established in the marketplace or replaced by new technology before becoming widely accepted.

To record your project on a CD-ROM, you need software to apply the proper parameter during the recording process. This is so that your CD-ROM will work in any player on any computer. When you create your

Figure 7–3. CD-ROM recorders are affordable and can be used to produce audio CDs as well.

project, you use the authoring program software to implement playing and previewing your project. Within the makeup of the finished CD-ROM must be an "execute" program, which allows it to be played but does not allow anyone to modify its structure. Versions of this software come with most CD-ROM recorders or authoring software. It walks you through the process, guiding you step by step. You'll be amazed at how little time it takes.

AVOIDING THE PITFALLS

You can avoid the pitfalls, but it's a little bit tricky and you'll probably have to try a few times before you get it all right. For one, you need to make sure the CD has all of the information it needs. Things like the animations, background screens, and .avi's, which come from outside sources like another CD-ROM, must be placed in something like an "extras" folder on your CD, so that each image or piece of video is available and can be inserted where it needs to go.

Another surprise is that fonts are drawn not from your CD-ROM but from the host computer; that is, the end user's computer playing back your CD-ROM. This is because many fonts are copyrighted by their designers and duplication of them in published form such as on your CD-ROM can get sticky. To get around this, authoring software is designed so that the finished CD-ROM will pull its fonts from the host computer. You'll find it's safest to stick with resident system fonts found on virtually all computers, fonts like Aerial or Helvetica. To display special fonts, it can be best to create them as a graphic element, displayed just like any other image.

Still another common mistake made by amateur CD-ROM designers is screen size. The most common screen resolution found on personal computers today is 800 × 600 pixels. This infers that the screen size of the viewer's monitor is 15 inch or larger. About one third of all computer owners use 14-inch monitors, which cannot display at 800 × 600 pixels but are limited to a resolution of 640 × 480. A CD-ROM page designed at 800 × 600 will be almost a third larger at 640 × 480. So, unless you are careful graphic elements and words will be pushed off the edge of the screen, changing your look entirely. The opposite can happen, too. A screen designed at 640 × 480 is reduced in size when viewed at a higher resolution. If you have inserted very small fonts or graphics at the 640 × 480 resolution, they may be difficult to read or view clearly when shrunk down at high resolution. The best option is to create your screens at 800 × 600 but change your monitor setting periodically and check how they appear at 640 × 480. A properly designed screen layout should look good in either mode.

CD-ROMs can be used in many different ways, as a digital photo album, an electronic informational brochure, or a playback medium for music videos. You can create custom music CDs, compilations, or your favorite tunes. One of the hottest new uses for CD-ROMs is as a training device. The "script" is written so that users can answer multiple choice or true/false questions, with the right or wrong answer leading them to the next level or back for study. Whatever your use or need, consider adding CD-ROMs to your video abilities.

WHAT ABOUT DVD?

In essence, digital video disks (DVD) is the same thing only different, another type of disk-based media with greater storage capacity. The main difference is that, as of this writing, consumer-level DVD recording gear is simply unavailable and the possibility of its use still is several years away. When the time comes, rest assured that the overall concept would be the same: Dedicated software translates video programs and runs them through a compression scheme that records the information to the DVD format. Build your experience now, and if DVD makes a lasting impact, eventually it should be within your grasp.

Your Video on TV

8

The tools of desktop video really open the doors to television and your ability to produce programs and shows. Exploring TV's possibilities can be a hobby or a new career, from cable access at night or on weekends to a full-time job as a producer of commercials, local programming, and even the possibility of working your way into national broadcast. If you're in it for the glory and not the money, then the only limit is your imagination and initiative.

HOW TO PRODUCE COMMERCIALS WITH YOUR CAMCORDER AND COMPUTER

Every day thousands upon thousands of commercials are shown on our TVs, and the number is growing constantly. Why? Because people with inexpensive, computer-based desktop video editing systems are making low-cost commercials for local businesses (see Figure 8–1). Today's desktop production studio can crank out pretty sophisticated, high-quality videos

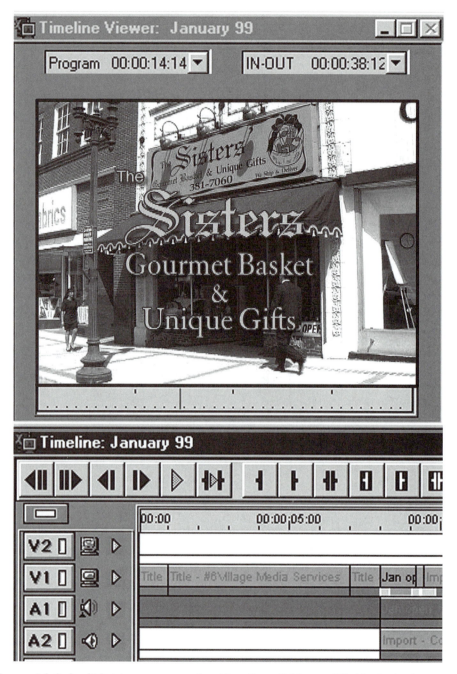

Figure 8–1. Commercials for local television are a very real and lucrative outlet for your PC video productions.

for a fraction of what the big guys charge. The business and the money are out there, the question is, "What does it take to get them?"

Major Leagues, Minor Leagues

Start out by knowing your limitations. Most national commercial spots for burgers, coffee, and other products are shot on film not video. Film is still superior in color and depth, and corporations with millions in their advertising budget pull out no stops to make their commercial look like you could reach out and touch someone. For 30 seconds of finished production it is not uncommon for these folks to spend well over $100,000.

Down a notch are what still would be considered major players. They shoot on Betacam, and charge possibly from $10,000 to $30,000 to get spinning 3D logos, shimmering video quality, maybe a celebrity spokesperson.

This is where the shake-up begins. As much as these big production houses would like to separate themselves, the bottom line is that the little person with a desktop video system is cutting a serious wedge into the production houses' business. The lines are blurring between professional and consumer, creating an entirely new category: the prosumer, the desktop video entrepreneur. Armed with high-resolution formats like Hi8, S-VHS, and digital (now even Betacam is affordable), coupled to a powerful desktop computer, the small independent is able to accomplish what for years was the exclusive domain of production studios with $100,000 (or more) edit suites.

Chances are you won't be making commercials for national broadcast TV. Your ticket to producing commercials is going to be local, perhaps local broadcast but more than likely on cable. Why? Because local broadcast affiliates, even though they must duke it out with dozens of other networks for an audience, still capture the biggest percentage of viewers. Therefore the cost of commercial airtime is going to be higher, limiting them to advertisers with deeper pockets. Exceptions are the smaller independent UHF stations and late-night time slots. This time is sold much cheaper than prime time and will attract a number of advertisers with a wide variety of things to sell.

Another reason you'll have a hard time breaking into broadcast television is that the network affiliates almost always have their own production studios and will be your competitor for the potential advertiser. But that doesn't leave you out cold. Chances are you can undercut them on the cost of production. The advertiser who has its own commercial, purchasing only airtime, most likely will pay less than one who is buying time and needs production work as well.

Cable opened the doors for the small producer of commercials. Instead of three or four networks, cable has dozens of channels, all with commercials. A cable company can sell ad time to niche markets, using networks like ESPN to reach male viewers, Lifetime for female audiences, MTV for the youth—the list goes on and on. Because the audience is smaller, ad time sells for less, making it more affordable for a greater number of businesses.

For a cable company to place local commercials on national cable networks, it must have in place channel insertion equipment. This consists of a VCR (usually 3/4 inch) linked to a computer and some sophisticated switching equipment. When the cable channel goes to a commercial break, coded signals in the network transmission turn on the insertion equipment and the process begins. The computer has a log identifying all the commercials on its "play tape" so that it can locate the proper commercial to be played at that specific time. The computer program allows the cable operator to sell prime-time spots for more money than off time. A printout verifies when the commercial aired, so those paying for time can be sure they're getting their money's worth. The around cost for one of these setups starts at $4000, and you need one for each channel. Small cable systems may have three or four such setups, mid-sized systems up to a dozen. The only limit is the cable company's investment and how much airtime it can sell.

Your main niche is the local business, the mom and pop or single-owner operation, companies not affiliated with a national chain. They need advertising to compete and they want it done in a low-cost manner, with big bucks results. You'll also encounter the occasional franchise owner who has "co-op" dollars from the main office to spend on advertising. Enter the new age video entrepreneur, armed with the latest gear and a desire to succeed at work that can be so much fun, you'll have to pinch yourself every once in a while exclaiming, "They actually pay me to do this."

Producing the 30-Second Commercial

It's amazing what you can do with 30 seconds. It goes by really quick, but there is plenty of time to bore viewers so they switch channels. Certain criteria almost always must be followed in every commercial you produce. That these details probably seem pretty obvious doesn't reduce their significance or that they can be easy to overlook. Sometimes satisfying the customer takes precedent over producing a high-quality commercial, think of all of the corny used car ads and business owners stammering, stiff as a board, performances that so clearly identify a local ad.

Generally speaking the company's name must be repeated as often as possible. The advertisers are paying for one thing: customer name recognition. Fairly early in the spot the name should be established, what company this commercial is about. Then it has to be repeated at the end, leaving the last imprint. If possible, mention it a time or two during the course of the narration or voice-over, reinforcing the name in the customer's mind.

Of course the advertiser's phone number follows suit and probably the address. Viewers must know how to contact your client and find their location. The phone number generally will be included at the end, the key is to have it on the screen long enough to imprint or be copied down if the viewer is so inspired. Two seconds is not really long enough. Five seconds will do. You may have it on the bottom of the screen for the entire commercial or somewhere in the middle and then again at the end.

If the client is a place of business, then usually you want to include a storefront shot. This makes a good closing shot with the graphics (address and phone number) superimposed. It can also be good for an opener, or establishing shot.

Using Psychology

Psychology plays a certain role both in the viewer's reaction and the client's satisfaction. Why do car dealers always want to do their own commercials? The answer is face recognition. It doesn't matter that the commercials are hokey or the dealers uncomfortable on camera and fodder for jokes by stand-up comedians. The dealers know that people will see them and when they come in to buy, that recognition from being on TV gives them an edge. People will ask for them by name.

You can use the same approach when shooting furniture stores, banks, just about any client. The people don't necessarily have to speak on-camera. You can have the employees smiling at the camera, going about their work, basically appearing on the TV screen, where their friends and relatives can see them. For weeks afterward, people will be coming in their place of business saying, "We saw you on TV." And that's what you want, people seeing the commercial. How else does the advertiser know that its commercial is working? It can run a sale, but print advertising will probably back it up. When people come in and comment on the commercial, then the advertiser knows that the ad is working, people are seeing it.

This same concept can be extended to the real heartstrings activator: kids. When the advertisers have their own children as "actors" in the commercial, they really are hooked. They beam with pride and get a real charge every time the ad appears. Here it is not so much whether the ad increases their business, but whether clients are happy with the spot and will advertise again.

If your advertiser has the right personality, humor in your commercial can be a real winner. The "plot" can be cornball, but still it will stick in people's minds, tickle their funny bones, and bring comments to the advertiser for years to come. Find a suitable performer by using one of the local colorful figures from an FM radio station as the on-camera talent, which provides face and name recognition as well as someone used to hamming it up. They don't always charge a whole lot for their time, because it gives them local exposure as well.

Here are a couple of examples of simple humorous ads. For a furniture store, start out with the actor's chair collapsing under him, and he has to go shopping for a new one. In the closing shot the actor is blissfully asleep in a comfortable recliner being loaded in a delivery truck. For a financial planner, while an investment brokers explains annuities to another person out on the golf course, a ball strikes her in the head. Collapsed on the ground, glasses askew, she speaks at the camera, saying to come see her in the office to learn more. When so many commercials are bland formula repeats, the humorous touch can really stand out and be remembered.

Tempo

To keep the viewers' attention, you must stimulate their senses. The main way you do this is with interesting video. Use movement in your shots, either from the figures on camera or by moving the camera itself. Instead of a simple pan, pan and then tilt the camera up. Study other commercials as a template. You'll see that something is moving in every shot. People are walking toward the camera or across the screen. If the scene is static then the camera moves.

Use lots of edits. Three seconds is about as long as you may want to stay on any one image, other than at the end for the closer. Some edits may be even less than 3 seconds. It is amazing how fast the mind can register, determine what is to be seen, and be ready for something else. Numerous edits keep the energy up and save you from boredom. You don't have to go to MTV extremes, but remember that the TV watchers of today have a lot of things competing for their attention. You have to match speed with the competition.

Acquiring High-Quality Images

The secret to producing "broadcast"-quality images with a consumer camcorder is lighting. All video cameras do better with proper lighting, and it is especially critical with single-chip camcorders. If you take the time to add extra lighting, including fill lights to eliminate shadows, bounce lighting to brighten faces without overexposure, all of this will work to your advantage by giving you professional results. Even a simple camera-mounted light can turn video that doesn't really cut it into an image that works.

The best way to check your lighting is by setting up a monitor on location. With a TV connected to your camcorder, you can see exactly what you are getting and adjust the lights until you get a picture that looks good. You can record a little bit, then do a playback to check all systems and see how the video reproduces from the tape.

You need to consider audio. Your commercial may consist of a narrator and music, with no live sound, in which case the on-location microphone is not a factor. However, if the people on-camera are speaking, you need to get away from the camera-mounted mike. A lapel or lavaliere mike works good for one person. A "shotgun" or zoom mike works best when recording a small group with several people speaking. With a "man on the street" interview style, a handheld mike will work. Wireless mikes can be a plus if the person on-camera is moving around. The complete kit has them all, a videographer ready for anything.

Editing Hardware and Software

Today's desktop video-equipped computers can perform all the editing functions, including special effects. The better your graphics, the more chance you'll have at producing commercials that will meet with approval and bring in more business. The computer is a fully functional character generator, perfect for any titles you'll need in your commercial productions. Use a scanner and art program to enter company logos, layering them over the video. Your computer, armed with the right software, can become a chroma key or luminance key, as well as generate wipes and transitions to bring logos on the screen in flips, swoops, and digital moves that let the client feel like they are getting a professional job.

You almost always have to transfer the finished product to an industrial format like 3/4 inch or Beta SP. Fortunately you can pick up used 3/4-inch gear for sometimes as little as a couple hundred dollars. Delivering the commercial on a professional format will open doors that otherwise would stay closed.

STARTING YOUR OWN CABLE SHOW

Starting your own cable TV show can be fun, challenging—and lucrative. With the onset of direct-broadcast satellites offering cable television companies stiff competition, these city-bound programming suppliers are pulling out their trump card in a high-stakes game with the audience as the prize. The one thing that cable can offer that the new satellite-delivered services cannot is locally produced programming. More than just the weather and news, video entrepreneurs and amateur producers are discovering that cable is a natural outlet for their creative energies. The door opens in many ways. The key is to find a niche, a way that will allow you to become a producer of real television, right in your hometown.

Getting Your Foot in the Door

You probably already have heard about cable access, but that's really only one way to create your own cable show, and it usually comes with one very big limitation: your show must be commercial free. Public access television can be a lot like the public broadcast system, in that it often is set up as a nonprofit so that more people have the opportunity to participate. But in many ways this system can hinder your ability to enter the production world. After all, the equipment costs a lot of money and shooting and editing takes time. Video production can be an expensive hobby unless you figure out a way for it actually to make you money.

Many cable systems have channels dedicated to local programming, but time on that channel can be purchased. Prices will vary depending on the city you live in, ranging from somewhat expensive to incredibly affordable. That's OK. This cost of programming time is the foundation you need to get started. It becomes part of the overhead for pulling off your project. What you need to make it work are sponsors.

Advertisers are the key to many types of media. From newspapers and magazines to broadcast TV, advertisers pay the bills. What do advertisers want? A guaranteed audience. They need to know that their offer, be it for products or services, is seen and heard by their target audience, the people they would like to have as customers. If you can deliver that audience, you can sell advertising. Sell enough advertising and you have a production budget.

What does it cost to buy airtime? That depends on many things, from the power of your negotiation skills to the hunger of the cable company for local programming. Prices start at absolutely free and go up from there. In many cases local producers actually receive free airtime at prime-time hours because they will draw viewers and subscribers for the cable service.

This is one place where the small-town producer has it over the folks in the big city. Because the audience is so much smaller, the competition can be virtually nonexistent. Even if the cable service charges a small fee, it is very likely to be less than $100 a week for a 30-minute to 1-hour slot. Can you sell $100 worth of advertising? The answer is a resounding *yes*—if you have the right attraction.

One Ticket for Admission—Local Sports

No question about it, America loves sports. Actually, that love is worldwide. But when it comes to catching the games of the home high school team, spirit can run especially high. Until recently one had to go to the game in person or perhaps listen on the radio. Not anymore. Hometown sports has been the answer for many video entrepreneurs seeking to enter television production (Figure 8–2). Parents, grandparents, teachers, alumni, students—a lot of people will tune in to watch the home team, especially if it is having a winning season.

You can deliver that audience to your local merchants. You'll find quite a number of businesses, such as car dealers, furniture stores, or restaurants, would be interested in having their advertising shown just before the game begins, at halftime, time-outs—you get the idea.

To do it right, you need to build up your kit. After all, the better your show, the more it will be watched and the more you can charge for advertising. A wireless mike or a direct mike placed on the announcer can provide your audio. You might be able get your audio from a radio if a local station is covering the game, provided you have permission.

Figure 8–2. Sports scores. Many people break into video production by providing coverage for local high school sports.

You want at least two camcorders, so you have more than one angle to show. The truly outfitted rig uses a video switcher and monitor console, linked headphones for communication to the camera operators, a desktop video computer loaded with player statistics, animated graphics, and station IDs, identifying your program, future air dates, and a last salute to your sponsors. These features can be added over time, as your budget allows.

The Home Show

Another programming phenomena taking root throughout the country is the real estate show (Figure 8–3). Realty agents have been using video for years, occasionally doing some editing and production, but more often presenting basic home video when displaying their properties. People are

Figure 8–3. The real estate show is a common locally produced program.

always moving, buying, or selling, which means there is a constant audience interested in watching a program showcasing properties for sale.

The real estate show adds the element of professionalism in that it assembles the homes much as a magazine ad would, displaying their various features and the desirable aspects of the home, with greater opportunity to show as well as tell. Because the profit potential from real estate can inherently turn over large funds of capital, good marketing increases the bottom line and creates a cash flow for advertising and marketing. A program that displays local homes for sale, which itself is promoted through other traditional advertising media (print, radio), can be a feather in the cap for the agent seeking additional residences to list.

While the realty company stands to greatly benefit from this exposure, it is not the only business interested in this type of program. Everyone in the home industry—the banks, the lumber and building materials suppliers, furniture dealers—can be courted as potential sponsors who would receive 30–60-second advertising spots within the program.

Of course you have to put together a production. Figure on a standard opening and closing for your show, as well as breaks where you give advice or information on shopping for a new home. Begin with a 30-second opener that follows the axiom, Tell them what your going to tell them. Give the name of the show, which of course identifies the real estate company. Talk a bit about the wonderful homes the viewer is going to see.

The bulk of the show will be a catalog of homes. With 1–2 minutes per property, you'll have quite a lot of material. Put together your segments for each home in consistent lengths (30 or 60 seconds works well) so that properties can be removed easily as they are sold and new ones inserted.

You may find it works for the Realtor to provide video footage of various homes. Give them a shot list, identifying standard views (front, back, the yard) followed by a list of interior shots, with an "other" category for special features such as a pool, nearby school, or additional buildings, like a barn. Instruct the person to use a tripod, and unless the camera has a fluid head, have him or her stick to straight, still shots without a lot of panning or zooming. A simple shot with good composition is better than video with movement if it is jerky and distracting.

Use your computer's character generator to give each house an ID number. Superimpose graphics of the Realtor's phone number and logo on the screen. Add a narrator's voice describing the home, and some light background music gives everything a smooth cohesive feeling.

It's a Living

Your biggest competitor in all of this could be the cable company itself. It is in the TV business and often will develop sophisticated edit facilities to churn out commercials as well as its own programming, aimed at attracting local viewers and of course sponsors.

Then again, some folks have figured out a job at the cable company can be a way to get their hands on the really nice toys of desktop video. Perks include interviews with visiting celebrities, politicians, trips to faraway places, and a status about town as "that guy on cable." A little knowledge of video, editing, and a spark of creativity can be the credentials you use to launch a new career or at least a fun job.

Will a show on cable work for you? Video is out there and happening in new and different ways, waiting to be discovered and explored. Your career will depend on the cable company, the cost of airtime, your skills as a salesperson as well as in production, no matter whether you are selling yourself, your ideas, or the block of time allocated for sponsors on your show. If you are a small producer who does weddings or perhaps the occasional industrial video, income from a cable show can be another source of cash, a way to use your system, your talents, and generate another payment on your latest equipment.

The important thing is to create a program that works efficiently, with a reasonable amount of labor relative to your profit. Planning a program and designing it to make money will make it fun and give you the desire to continue.

SHOOTING THE INFOMERCIAL

We've all seen those late-night sell-a-thons commonly called *infomercials.* Part entertainment, part commercial, infomercials usually last anywhere from 3 to 30 minutes and are used to sell products and services via a format that takes time to get the viewer involved, making it possible to use a softer sell approach than the impact necessary in a 30-second commercial.

Once the domain of late night national broadcast and cable networks, infomercials increasingly are finding there way into smaller local broadcast and cable systems as well as other outlets such as direct-mail distribution or point-of-sale videos. Most cable companies have at least one channel dedicated to local production, the channel for high school sporting events, town government meetings, and now the local infomercial. This change has opened the door for small, independent producers armed with a camcorder and some basic editing tools. Here are several examples, ideas that you can emulate in your own area to generate some much needed cash for even more video toys—I mean tools.

The Car Lot

Here's an infomercial that just about drives itself, a technique you could use for a local car dealer. Placed your camcorder on a tripod with the salesperson positioned in the right-hand portion of the screen, framed for a medium closeup. As he or she talks to the camera, in the background to the screen left have various other salespeople drive a car or truck into the camera's view and stop. The on-camera spokesperson can introduce the driver, describe the vehicle a little bit (starting, of course, with the make, model, and year), and add a few choice tidbits of information, such as that it was a one-owner car or had low mileage.

Back at the computer, add some simple titles at the beginning over a background shot showing the dealership and its sign. Insert some commercials, break up the car parade into segments, and before you know it, you have a show.

The Interview

Another type of common infomercial is the interview (Figure 8–4). It takes someone to ask questions, allowing the person being interviewed to respond and describe the products or services he or she provides. A good deal of the production can be done in a single camera shoot, first videoing the subject, then shooting the interviewer separately, asking questions and looking interested, amused, or concerned. It doesn't matter that the "cutaway" shots are videoed after the actual interview. When edited into the final production, the audience will never know the difference.

To keep the show interesting, sometimes the owner is outfitted with a wireless mike for a behind-the-scenes atmosphere. This helps to give the piece a documentary feel. The format works well for a local business, since

Figure 8–4. The interview is one of the most common forms of video production, from news to advertising.

the viewers may recognize the company, become curious, and watch. Because the production is kept very simple, the business owner can put together a 15-minute show for virtually the same production costs of a more intensely edited 30-second commercial. The extra time really lets the person tell his or her story and get across lots more detailed information.

These are just some of the ways you can get in the infomercial game. Really, any video production designed to inform and sell can be considered an infomercial. Commonly referred to as *industrial* or *marketing videos,* the concept is in many ways the same: make it entertaining, informative, and inspire the viewer to action—to purchase a product or hire a specific company for the service and expertise they can provide.

Building Your Own Video Website

9

No question about it, the Internet is where it's happening today. The convergence of computer and video technologies and the Internet represents the new frontier in communication. Over the next several years we will see an increasing use of the Internet as a medium for video, from teleconferencing to soap operas. Already we have live concerts over the Internet every week. Network news stories can be played back at your convenience, and an increasing number of sites feature the cyber equivalent of TV advertising.

How can you put your video on the Internet? It is easier than you think. With the right software and computer hardware, you can create a website with full-motion video right now. You can send v-mail, video clips with sound, as attachments to your regular e-mail. Even more fantastic, you can use your computer system for live, real-time, video–audio chats and business conferences—the communications promise of the future here today. Amaze your friends, enhance your business, and ride the wave of cybervideo into the next century.

GETTING A SITE

First you'll need a place on the Internet to call home, a domain (Figure 9–1). Many ISPs (Internet service providers) give their subscribers a small amount

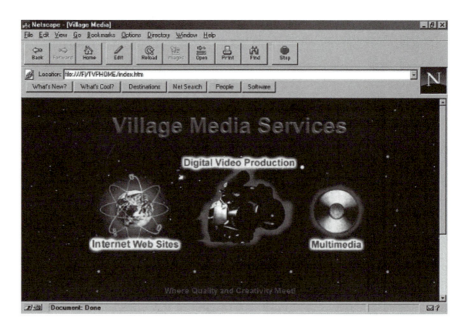

Figure 9–1. The Village Media website. The first step in creating a website is to establish a domain.

of space for users to create a home page. However, with prices plummeting for space on a server, those seeking to set up a dedicated URL (universal resource locator) go through the steps of registering a domain name and establishing an actual address. Registering your name will cost around $100 (a biannual fee) and of course it has to be a name that no one else is using or has registered. You can do a quick check by simply typing in the desired address name and see if anyone else already has a site by that name. If this check doesn't turn up anything, there are sites on the Web that will do a more thorough check in case the name has been registered but is inactive. Most companies that lease space for domains will do the registration process for you as part of their service.

FROM DREAM TO REALITY

Once you have a domain set up you need to create a basic site. To do this you need a web editor (Figure 9–2). Today's web editing and design programs eliminate the need to work in HTML coding.

The process of creating your site in many ways is similar to working with a document layout and design program. Begin with a clean page, then fill it up with titles, paragraphs, images, animation, and movies. Choose a solid color background or tile an image pattern (Figure 9–3). Just remember it is "background" and should not overpower or distract from the main content.

Type in words as with a word processor and add attributes such as bold or italic and make them large or small as you desire. Choose different fonts, but keep in mind that displayed fonts are chosen by the end user's computer. Your website communicates the basic content and the computer owned by the person exploring your site creates the text. This means that, if you choose a font that is not resident in the user's computer, it will substitute something else in its place, which can drastically alter the look of your site. So, to avoid this, use only fonts that are common to virtually every computer, such as Arial, Times Roman, or Helvetica.

A site with all words is pretty boring, so most people dress up their pages by adding pictures. Numerous CD-ROM collections contain generic artwork and such, but for original imagery you have to start from scratch. Draw your own in an art or paint program, import photos with a scanner, or

Figure 9–2. Macromedia Dreamweaver.

do frame grabs from your video using an installed video card and the right video software.

Once you have done a "frame capture" or turned a piece of video into a still image, save it in a format that the Internet can use, either .gif (Figure 9–4) or .jpeg. The Compuserve .gif format was designed specifically for use on the Internet. It uses a limited palette of 256 colors, which helps keep down the file size for faster downloading. It is ideal for flat images, like titles or cartoons, that don't have a lot of shading or color variation.

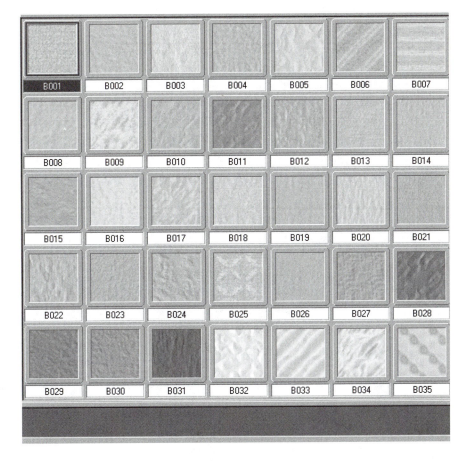

Figure 9–3. Examples of background texture (see color insert).

Figure 9–4. The .gif image file format has a restricted color palette of only 256 colors and is best suited to flat logos and cartoon images (see color insert).

Full-color images call for the .jpeg format, which uses a special type of compression to squeeze pictures with lots of content into a small file. Ideally the file size of an image should be 50K or less, because this is what will make your images display faster on the viewer's screen. Keep your image dimensions small and take advantage of programs designed to super-streamline your files without compromising image quality. Examining a side by side comparison of the original and the streamlined image allow you to judge how far you can reduce the file size before the image starts to degrade. You can convert a 72K image file to as less than 10K and still have a decent looking picture.

ADDING MOVEMENT

Still images are your mainstay on a website, but any movement you can add is true eye candy. Netscape has its streaking meteors, other sites have blinking words, spinning atoms, animation that adds flavor and spice.

The easiest and most common way to add an animation is in the form of an animated .gif. This is simply a series of .gif images played back in succession (Figure 9–5), usually in the neighborhood of 5–15 frames a second, substantially less than the 30 frame a second rate for standard NTSC video.

Numerous programs create simple .gif animation. An easy way to get started is to use one still image for the beginning frame and another for the end frame. The animation program then can fill in all the frames in between, creating a wipe between the two, such as a venetian blind effect or an opening from the center. If you are up to the challenge, create a series of drawings from scratch, frame by frame.

JAVA AND DYNAMIC HTML

Software designers and programmers are on a constant competitive course to develop methods to add movement to websites with a minimal amount of load time. Again the user must have a current browser, and in some cases, it may be necessary to download additional software that works as a plug-in, enhancing the browser's capability. Often the plug-in is incorporated into

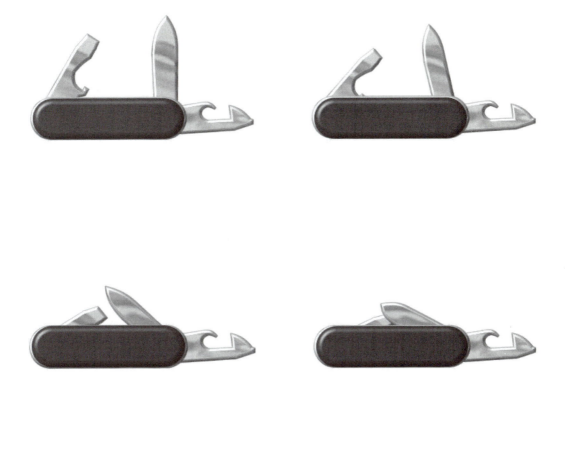

Figure 9–5. Example of 10-frame .gif animation.

new releases of Netscape and Microsoft Explorer, so that the web surfer can immediately benefit from the latest developments.

Still another approach is to develop a new programming language, as is the case with Sun Microsystem's Java. This cross-platform scripting allows the web designer to take advantage of stock Java appletes, programs with Java animation that can be customized by the end user. Java's revolutionary approach is being adapted to many different applications, beyond websites and into all manner of computer-controlled technology.

Dynamic HTML, enables you to create simple animation and changing images using code (JavaScript) built right into the website. A design feature of the more sophisticated web editing programs is to tie many predefined behaviors into your links. For example, when the person visiting your site allows their cursor to pass over a hot button, the image underneath might change, attracting attention to the link.

Note that older browsers such as Netscape 2 or Internet Explorer 3.0 are unable to utilize dynamic HTML commands. In most cases they just won't respond. As more and more people upgrade to the newer browsers, this becomes less of an issue. Because having these extra bells and whistles can be what helps your site stand out, you'll probably want to take advantage of the capability.

PAGE LAYOUT

Layout in website design can seem a bit confusing at first, as you figure out how images and text are aligned on the screen. The primary technique used by most basic page designers involves tables (Figure 9–6). Tables typically are seen as boxes tied together in rows and columns. The size and shape of each table cell can be modified as well as the relative dimensions to the overall screen. Tables usually are made transparent, enabling you to control placement and location of text and graphics while keeping the confining boundaries invisible to the casual website visitor.

Dynamic HTML expands your layout options with Layering, which lets you overlap images and text. Layers can be stacked, nested together, and arranged in any order. Again you have to be careful that people with older browsers may not see your page as you intended.

Another design element to consider is the ability to work with multiple frames (Figure 9–7). Have you ever visited a site where the main screen

Figure 9–6. Adobe Pagemill with table divisions. Tables are used to define position and layout for your web page. Table cells, invisible when displayed on the Internet, are indicated by the dotted lines.

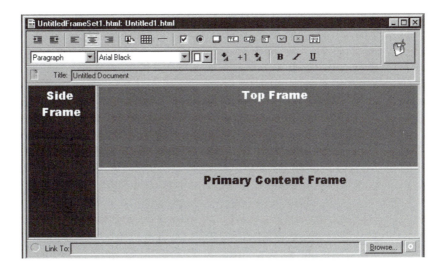

Figure 9–7. A single web page can be divided into a combination of multiple frames, each displaying different content.

content changes but the menu bar stays in place the whole time? This is because the site was designed using multiple frames. The web page you create is known as a *frame.* You can create frames of varying sizes and display several simultaneously on the screen. Typically you see extra frames across the top of the screen or down the left side, maybe both, so you could be looking at three different frames at once. Together they are called a *FrameSet.* Setting them up is a little more involved than just working with one frame, but you'll find that your web editing program will make it easy and intuitive.

INTERNET VIDEO—THE NEXT LEVEL

One of the most exciting frontiers on the Internet is the addition of real-time audio and video. More than 150,000 hours of live content are produced every week. Over 1000 radio stations and TV stations broadcast live and air programming on the Web.

Because video uses images from real life, file sizes generally are much larger than typical .gif animation. You can convert your .avi and quick-time movies to animated .gif for playback; and while that will work with a minimum amount of effort in front, the cost is the extreme amount of download time. It can take several minutes to download a movie that may last only 10–15 seconds. Therefore anyone serious about displaying video on the 'Net opts to use special software that compresses the video files then decompresses them a little at a time during playback.

The most common way to play video via the Internet is for the viewer or web surfer to first download specific video player software (Figure 9–8), which is compatible with the video clip the user would like to see. This player software is downloaded onto the visitor's computer as a plug-in, and once installed on the hard drive, it will activate anytime the user visits a site set up to use it.

The buzzword for all this is *streaming,* which takes the video information and feeds it to computers in "bytes" the computer can swallow. Think of the video or audio content from a website as a lake stored on the hard drive of a host computer or server. A flow of water, video and audio information, continuously pours over the dam that is the phone line to the modem and computer. As the information pours past, more will replace it,

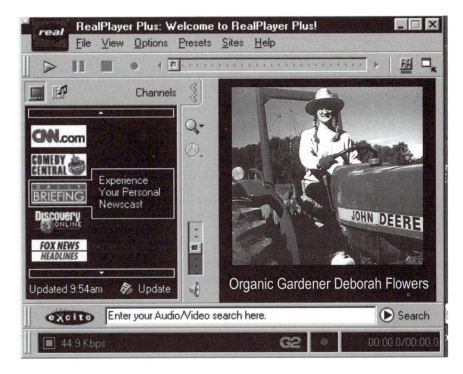

Figure 9–8. To play streaming video files on your browser, you must have a compatible media player, like the RealPlayer Plus shown here.

a constant stream of real-time information. Without streaming software, a computer is forced to first download the entire media file before playback. Streaming gets playback started faster, a sort of virtual real time.

Videos are composed of single frames or images, which are viewed in rapid succession, one after another. Streaming creates a buffer that stores the first few frames in a cached memory. Playback then begins from the stored information while, at the same time, gathering new frames into the buffer to replace what already has been shown. The streaming software calculates just how much information the computer can handle and sends that amount and no more. When everything is working as it should, the result is real-time video and audio, almost more of a trickle than a stream, passing from a website to a computer.

WHAT IS A PLUG-IN?

Basically a plug-in is an extra piece of software added to a computer to expand its capability. Probably the most common type of plug-in to an Internet browser is the media player, which makes it possible to play video and audio files from the Internet without first downloading them into your computer. To hear or view a media file, the user must have a copy of the correct player software residing on his or her computer. Without the proper player on the system, generally the user will be instructed to go to the media player website to download the software, a process that can take several minutes. Next the user must install the player program by locating its file on the computer's hard drive and running it through a setup procedure.

One slight problem with plug-ins can stem from efforts made to improve their performance. Software is constantly being updated, and it stands to reason that a file created using a 5.0 version of an audio or video recording program will need a similar 5.0 player to play back on your computer. Web surfers with 2.0 players are simply out of luck until they download the latest version of the player software. Another obstacle can be the number of different, proprietary multimedia player systems in use, each requiring its own download.

There are several different approaches for solutions to this problem in the web world. Microsoft has attempted to develop a single player compatible with virtually all other media player plug-ins, however, it still is incompatible with some versions. Another common option is to supply the plug-in invisibly to the web viewer, embedding the player into the website itself. Some companies have succeeded in making the multimedia player file so small that it can be downloaded to the viewer's computer in under a minute, without the user even realizing this is happening. After a short wait the file begins playing on its own, and to the viewer, it appears as if no plug-in was required.

GETTING YOUR VIDEO AND AUDIO ON THE WEB

To make your audio .wav files and your video .avi and .mov files ready to upload to the Web you must have a publishing program (Figure 9–9). The publishing program you use will be determined by the multimedia player plug-in system you want your viewers' to have on their systems. The

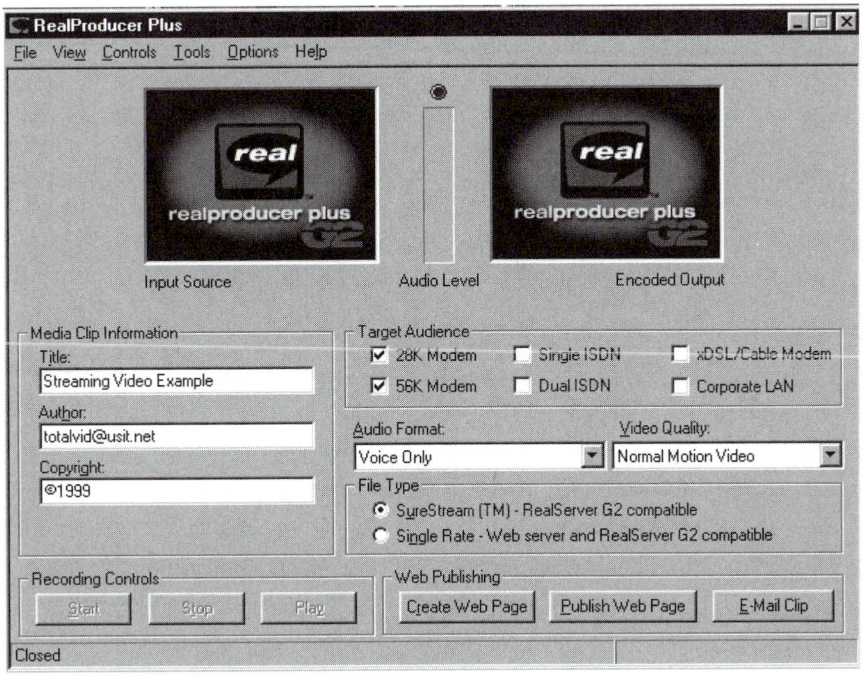

Figure 9–9. Convert your audio and video files to streaming media player files with an Internet video publishing program like Real Producer Plus.

publishing program imports your file, then automatically processes it for playback with its own player software. Most systems create a new proprietary file format, which must be uploaded to your website, along with a series of other proprietary player files, which also must be present for the system to work. You'll probably find it easiest to place all of the relevant files in a single folder on your website.

These files are linked to the rest of your website in more or less the same way that your .jpeg and .gif images, residing on your server. Part of your page design sends out a call for the player software to see if it is residing on the viewer's computer.

LIVE PERFORMANCE

Multimedia publishers also can be used to transmit live audio and video, such as from a radio station, TV station, or live concert. However, the processing is somewhat more complex and requires a moderately fast computer, at least 300 MHz or better is recommended. Camera and audio feed supply the source information, which is converted in real time by the publishing software, then uploaded to the Web. It's an amazing process, but not something for the video neophyte.

UNDERSTANDING THE LIMITS

Video on the Web has its limitations, particularly video quality. The object of the game is to make the most with what you have. First, it's important to identify your "target audience." In other words, decide what connection speed most of your audience will have. Faster modem speeds will process more data, important for high-quality video images and CD-quality audio, but you will lose people with older systems that cannot access your material.

Frame rates are usually cut in half or more to reduce file size and the amount of information that must be sent. The typical video with 30 frames a second is dropped down to 15, even 10, frames a second, which may produce staggered or strobelike movement of the images.

You can select the level of video quality. Some systems sacrifice resolution, again to reduce file size and permit faster viewing. Images can become pixelated and a bit blurry, like looking at something underwater, however, the form and movement are there and you get a general idea of the action taking place. By understanding the limits of the technology, you can define your videos for the best results. Here are some tips:

1. *Limit your movement.* To help reduce information overloads, .avi movies typically run at 15 frames a second, not 30 as in regular video. This tends to make them a bit choppy. Movement accentuates this difference; however, if the shot is of a person, sitting and talking to you on the screen without moving, the loss is barely noticeable.
2. *Stay big and bold.* The screen size is kept small to reduce the information overload, so detail gets lost. Closeups work best, like head and shoulders shots, as well as large bold graphics.

3. *Let your audio tell the story.* Audio is much easier to send intact over the Web, sharp and clear. If it carries the bulk of the information you wish to express and the video is used to reinforce that information, you will be happier with the results.

A BIT ABOUT BANDWIDTH

Bandwidth determines the amount of data that can be squeezed through an Internet connection and into your computer. The modem establishes one set of limitations. Modems are rated in the amount of data they can receive per second. Standard sizes include 14.4, 28.8, and 56 KBs (kilobytes per second). Obviously the higher the KBs, the more data it can handle. The Internet connection from the service provider is another gateway or possible limiting factor. When you dial in to an ISP, notice that the connection rate appears somewhere on the screen. It doesn't help to have a 56.6 modem if your phone line connection is only 28.8 or less.

V-MAIL, VIDEO CONFERENCING, AND THE INTERNETCAM

The heart and soul of this concept is the InternetCam, a camera linked to a computer via a video card that, when combined with a microphone, duplex audio card, and a connection to the Web, brings the Internet video experience to a new level. Liven up your e-mail by turning it into v-mail, video messages recorded quickly via the installed camera directly onto your hard drive then forwarded to friends, family, or business associates. These little .avi attachments add spice and a personal touch that standard e-mail often loses.

Perhaps even more exciting is the live conferencing and two-way chat capability that the InternetCam offers. It works like a video phone, permitting live, two-way conversations in which each person can see and hear the other as they talk. Whether used for business or family fun, the experience presents amazing possibilities.

Getting your InternetCam system running is fairly simple but does require a few pieces of special hardware and software. First, of course, is the camera and built-in microphone. You can use your camcorder, although many people prefer to use the inexpensive, dedicated cameras deigned strictly for such use. They're small and inexpensive, generally under $150. You need a PC with Windows 95 or 98 and a clock speed of 133 MHz or better. The specs call for 16 MB of RAM, but that's really a minimum these days for anything you might want to do. The software for capturing video will take up around 10 to 30 MB of space on your hard drive. Use your standard video capture and editing software for v-mail. Specialized programs are available to facilitate conferencing and video chats.

You need some dedicated hardware as well: a PCI or AGP video card (often packaged with the camera), plus a full-duplex audio card. Most new computers will have a duplex audio card but you need to make sure. Many older or lower-quality audio cards are simplex rather than duplex. Simplex audio is like a walkie-talkie, with only one person or sound able to be heard at a time. Duplex audio is like a telephone, where both parties can speak and be heard at the same time. This is what you want for your video phone.

The Internet may prove to be the biggest area for growth in video production. Fortunately your computer and its video-related software—the capture card to the nonlinear editor, painting and drawing programs to animators and music makers—all fit perfectly into the Internet landscape. Properly armed, the desktop video producer is positioned to be a true player, not just a passenger looking on but a high-speed driver along the legendary information highway.

Video Projects

10

You've got the full kit: the camcorder, the computer outfitted with a non-linear editing system complete with a full-frame video capture card, software that delivers multiple audio and video tracks, and eye-popping transitions—this puppy's ready to go to work. Now what you need are some simple projects to cut your teeth on.

You'll find it best to start out with something short, which can be accomplished quickly but still give you the satisfaction of following through from start to finish. There are several other reasons why this is a good idea. When digitizing to the hard drive, it can be easy to overload your system's capability, especially if your supply of RAM is limited. In the middle of digitizing a clip, your system may cough and sputter then display an "overload" message. To avoid this, keep your video clips, and therefore your shots, at under a minute. For most scenes this is no problem, since in the final edit you very seldom will stay on one camera angle for that long anyway.

You'll also find that very large productions (15 or 30 minutes or more) present an incredible amount of information for the computer to deal with. When you insert a new clip into a 30-minute project, everything on either side has to move over, necessitating an extraordinary amount of calculation to shift, yet still maintain all the relationships of titles, transitions, clips, and the rest.

THE PUBLIC SERVICE ANNOUNCEMENT

Every organization can use help getting out its message. The public service announcement (PSA) can be an excellent way to offer your services and gain experience. Although broadcast affiliates and cable companies are not in the business of giving away airtime, they almost always set aside some space for PSAs, if for nothing more than their own self-promotion. Securing this airtime may be a chore you take on or it may be best for a representative of the organization itself to make the contact.

Your PSA more than likely will be a 30-second or 60-second spot. It will need to cover the bases, providing the viewer with essential information such as the name of the group being presented and how to contact it. Other than that, the possibilities are wide open.

Also the organization you wish to assist may be more interested or in need of a 3–5-minute informational production, something that could be used for fund-raising or educating people about the work it does. This type project may call for more material to work with, but in some ways it can be easier to produce than a 30-second PSA, since you have no time constraints. Trying to communicate everything in a succinct 30 seconds can be a real challenge.

It all boils down to a script and storyboard. Will you interview the people of importance in the organization and let them have their say? Or will you use people to tell a story? Is there a call to action requiring the viewer to do something like write a congressional representative or make a donation? Will the actors speak or will you use voice-over, that is, a narrator? All of these decisions fall under planning, the best thing you can do to ensure a positive and successful production experience.

If this is truly your first or one of your first projects, apply the KISS rule— keep it simple. Interviews can work out best because there is only one person to light and mike for audio. The background can be a blank cloth, a wall enhanced with a plant, a finite area to illuminate rather than needing to deal with a whole room. Using your nonlinear editing system you can cut and paste the interviews to edit out the uhhhs and duhhhs, even rearrange words to help the subject communicate more clearly. Cover these edits with "cutaways," other video clips that serve as examples of what they are talking about.

Of course the interview will only work if the subject speaks well on camera. It also may not communicate the service of the organization or group as much as unrehearsed video of the people engaged in their primary activity. This might be a youth organization working with underprivileged kids or an environmental group planting trees, beautifying a park, or saving a whale. Here you head into the field with your camcorder, capturing as much interesting footage as you can.

Back at the edit suite review the material, select shots for the final production, and digitize them into the computer. Add voice-over narration, an easy way to get a more professional sound. One good source is local radio personalities, who may donate their services to help the cause.

These projects will draw on all your skills, from shooting to script writing. It will use every aspect of your nonlinear editing system, including the titler, transition effects, audio tracks, and blending in background music with live sound or narration.

These days everyone needs a website and this could turn out to be the best way for you to contribute your video computer skills to a nonprofit organization (Figure 10–1). Like a video production, you need to analyze

Figure 10–1. The PSA. Nonprofit groups provide a way for you to exercise your skills—and do some good at the same time.

the message to be communicated, organize the information into a logical sequence, and make it attractive. Give the group a little something extra like a short video movie, and you are bound to leave a lasting impression.

THE COMMERCIAL

A step to the right of the PSA is the commercial. Thousands of small, independent business owners are in your city, and chances are you know several. Do they advertise on television or cable? Granted the cost of production is small when compared to what they will pay for advertising time on a channel, still every little bit helps. You may have a friend that would be quite willing to save a few hundred dollars to get a commercial made. Do a good job, and the next time they call you could be ready to charge for your services. It also may open the door to other clients, business owners who like what they see and want you to make a commercial for them. This is one way to get the ball rolling.

THE MUSIC VIDEO

Music videos (Figure 10–2) are fun because they can be a place to let your creativity go wild. There are a few different ways to approach this type of production. First, what is the purpose of the video? Is it to promote a band or a singer? Or is it just for fun, with friends or perhaps your children lip-synching to a popular song?

Bands may want you to document their live performances. This has certain advantages, in that the artists have true feeling in their actions. Make sure there is sufficient stage lighting and not some dim mood lighting with tons of atmosphere that is impossible to capture on tape. The band or solo performer needs to be well lit. Hard shadows are OK, they just add to the drama of the performance.

One drawback, however, is the sound. It is almost impossible to get really good sound from a live performance. Professional music videos are produced using studio recordings and the band or performer pantomimes or lip-syncs the chosen song. Even all the people playing instruments mime, that is, act out their performance to match the previously recorded music.

Figure 10–2. Local musicians can be a creative way to get started on a video project.

When videoing the performers, a tape or CD is played from a boombox or stereo system off-camera so that the people involved know what notes to play, what words to sing. Funny as it sounds this is more or less how it's done most of the time.

Unless you are shooting with multiple cameras, you will need to work on the same song over and over so that the camera can shoot from many different angles. One take may focus on the singer, another the lead guitar solo. Other cutaway shots could concentrate on the other instruments, including closeups of hands, tapping feet, silhouettes, and more.

Of course, you can go beyond the performance music video to the more artistic version, with the performers in unusual locations or situations. In every case, the song is played through a stereo system so that everyone will move to the right beat and sing along with the words if necessary.

The big challenge for the music video is editing and this is where your nonlinear editor really comes through. First, lay down the music track. Then the key is to make your edits match or be right on the beat. Fortunately with nonlinear editing, there's undo. You can try over and over until you get it right, shaving off a frame here and there as need be. Editing to the beat is the real secret to a successful music video. Miss the beat and your audience will not get in the groove.

THE BIRTHDAY PARTY

Although you may have over 2 hours of little Timmy's birthday party on tape, there is really no reason why a tightly edited 3–5-minute version can't tell the whole story. In fact your audience will probably love you for it. Go for the highlights, like the last two lines of "Happy Birthday" followed by blowing out the candles. Don't show the opening of every gift, just one or two that were special. Add a few highlights of the games and fun after the cake has been devoured. Look for faces—of the birthday child, the proud parents, and grandparents. Be sure to include a few shots of brothers and sisters and best friends. Spice up the end with a video montage set to music showing scenes from past birthdays.

These are but a few possible projects that you can create with your computer video editing equipment, but they capture the essence of what you need to do for just about any editing production. Whether the goal of your video is to tell a story, preserve memories, get someone elected, or sell a product, the steps you take here will keep you on the right path. From this point forward every TV show, every movie, every commercial that passes before you is another tool for learning, to be analyzed and critiqued, studied, maybe even copied. Because manipulating the tools really is just the beginning. From here you must begin to develop your creative ability, learning production techniques that begin with good camera work and follow on through to the final edit decision. The benefits are many: personal satisfaction from a job well done, perhaps a lucrative new career. At the very least, it is an opportunity to exercise and flex your mind. As we rise to meet the challenge of learning new things, we stimulate our own sense of well-being and happiness, and perhaps this is all the reward we need.

Appendix

Software and Hardware Solutions

This is just a partial listing of the software and hardware available. Look to these as examples when deciding what to use when setting up a PC video system. With so many options to choose from and more appearing every day, it would be impossible to list them all. However, you will find this to be a comprehensive overview, giving you some idea of how various programs and hardware compare and the features each brings you.

LOW-COST VIDEO CARDS, FRAME AND VIDEO CAPTURE, AND SIMPLE NONLINEAR EDITING

InVideo/PCI

The InVideo/PCI system by Focus Enhancements is an inexpensive internal card system, street priced at under $200. The supplied CD-ROM contains all the necessary drivers and support software, so within minutes you'll have the whole system up and running. Operation is extremely simple. It uses ComputerEyes software for frame capture. Use the autocalibrate option to establish contrast and color balance, click on the Capture button for it to instantly grab a frame.

For video capture the InVideo/PCI system uses a different piece of software, CineMaker. The process essentially is the same but with more options. You can opt for audio capture or not, save it immediately to the hard drive or work in RAM, adjust frame rates, put a time limit on the digitizing, or define the video source (composite, NTSC, or PAL) and the compression rate.

A cute feature is the sequential frame capture, which lets you grab one frame at a time, but stack them one after the other. This is perfect for amateur animators. Grab a frame, make an adjustment, then grab another in succession. Claymation here we come.

Pinnacle's Studio 400

Pinnacle has video capture and editing hardware and software at many different levels of quality and price. Studio 400 is the first rung of the ladder, and it is an amazing little system. At the heart is an external video "mixer," which can send captured video to the hard drive or loop it through to a VCR for the tape to tape recording. This system has it all—edit control, storyboard and timeline editing, titles (200 styles), and transitions (over 100) as well as a library of music, courtesy of Sonic Desktop. It accepts S and composite video, and will capture single frames as well as video at 320×240 pixels (or smaller). The system is available through various mail order sources for under $200. You definitely get a lot of bang for the buck.

Pinnacle Systems, Inc.
280 N. Bernardo Avenue
Mountain View, CA 94043

VIDEO PRODUCTION NONLINEAR EDITING SOFTWARE

Avid MCXpress

Avid built its reputation in the broadcast world, and MCXpress brings most of these features and functions to the personal PC. It does everything you'd expect from a professional level nonlinear editor and in a clear and concise manner. Its tools are intuitive; its video quality and performance, excellent. Sold as a stand-alone or bundled in turnkey systems with a video card and disk drives, MCXpress is a serious tool for the video professional.

Two tracks of video and four audio tracks are displayed across the bottom of the edit window with random access to any point in time. You can preview videos clips at thumbnail-sized images or at full-screen size on a second NTSC monitor. Modify your edit decision list with an unprecedented 32 levels of Undo/Redo.

The MCXpress system comes with a limited number of special effects for A/B roll or transitions from one video clip to another: a variety of basic wipes, zooms, pushes, and squeezes as well as the all-important dissolve. The page peel is very nice, with video on both sides of the page, plus a sheen or reflection on the back side of the page, which adds a little more realism to the effect. Avid expanded the number of effects since the program's original release, by adding a transition series that includes things like exploding cubes and bouncing spheres. The special effects are virtually unlimited, because MCXpress will work with many third party software effects packages.

Built-in filter effects allow you to add texture like a mask over your video images for a different look. These range from the traditional posterization to neat options like blur, hue, and saturation control.

The system also includes PIP (picture in picture). You can zoom in the picture from barely visible to any size and control its path of travel. Another important feature is chrominance and luminance keying. The chroma key is adequate but others are better.

You can import animation created in other programs. Animation is treated as scenes in your production the same as any other video source. It can be combined with the chroma key to make flying logos appear over the top of other video. MCXpress is compatible with just about every file format out there, allowing you to import or export a variety of file types, such as .avi, .wav, .bmp, .jpeg, .tiff, .tga, and .omf.

An important feature of MCXpress is the batch capture, which allows you to go through your source tape, select in and out points of scenes, and leave the computer and VCR to relocate and digitize all your material into the computer. This initial digitization can be done at a low-resolution compression ratio to save disk space, then you can redigitize only the final source material necessary for the high-resolution on-line edit.

Convenience is added by the nesting multiple effects feature. Many times a finished or edited scene may comprise several layers of video. For example, the first layer would be the background video. Then there might be a PIP image, maybe two, floating or layered on top of the original background. Another layer might hold titles and graphics. Quite often in production work, the editor or the client will want a change after the layers have been rendered into one. The change might be to the wording of the title or to correct a misspelling. With the older software all you could do was remove all the layers and start over. With the nesting feature, MCXpress lets you separate the layers on the timeline. You then can change just one layer without affecting the others.

Considered a powerful, sophisticated PC-based nonlinear editor, MCXpress even has been used in the production of feature film documentaries. Its long established reputation makes this one of the most popular systems among serious industrial and professional video producers.

Fast Video Machine

Over the last several years, the Fast Video Machine has been making a name for itself in video circles as a special effects generator, a titler, an edit controller, and now as a nonlinear editor. Fast Video nonlinear editing comes in "lite" and full-blown packages, complete with video card and software, VCR control, and dynamic effects.

Media 100

One of the first nonlinear editing systems to be widely used is the Media 100. Originally a Mac-based system, it offers many options: entry-level and high-end systems, special effects, character generation, plus RGB component processing for working with Betacam or digital VCRs. The on-screen controls are straightforward and easy to understand. If you can handle basic computer operation, you can be up and running in no time. On the top half of the monitor, inset screens show you the video footage in a little window, while below that you see a graphic display of the edit decision list, complete with multiple audio tracks. Media 100 is well established as a broadcast quality tool.

CD-ROM

MacroMedia—Authorware and Director

Authorware by MacroMedia is specifically designed for creating CD-ROMs. You start with a blank timeline, then drag and insert various icons to create a diagram. There are icons for digital movies (.avi, animation), sound, and pictures. Navigation icons direct the flow. Wait icons add a pause between screens or instruct the user to press a Continue button when ready.

To streamline the diagram, the timeline icons can be grouped together under a single "map" icon. By drawing a square around the selected icons and selecting Group from the menu, the entire batch is enclosed inside the map icon, which can be opened to reveal the contents of this other level. As your program gets more complex, with multiple levels and directions, you may find the map icon a very useful tool.

Director, also by MacroMedia, has been used to create hundreds of CD-ROM programs and games. It simultaneously is both simple and extremely complicated, with an intuitive approach that becomes second nature once you get past the initial learning curve. In many ways Director has the feel of a video nonlinear editing system. Images are imported into the library, then placed on a timeline. There are two audio tracks and dozens of potential video layers. Next you add transitions and any navigational commands. Markers indicate starting and stopping points for loops or leaps from one point to another.

The various elements (graphics, animation) can be stacked and overlapped on the screen. You control what is sent to the back or brought to the front. The bottom layer would be the background. Next might be your primary images and informational text. Finally there will be your assortment of buttons, which are assigned various functions with direct script entry or through a library of commands that you can select.

MacroMedia
600 Townsend
San Francisco, CA 94103

ART PROGRAMS

Corel Draw and Corel Paint

For many years Corel has produced one of the primary art programs in the PC world. Its drawing and painting programs are but two of a whole range of products, all geared around manipulating images, including a vast library of CD-ROM images as well as a painting program, a 3D modeler, and an animation program.

When it comes to creating titles, font selection is paramount. Corel Draw (a vector-based program) adds to your arsenal by bringing along 1000 True Type and Type 1 fonts. However, keep in mind that having too many fonts stored in your hard drive can slow your programs, so add only the ones you need. Leave the rest on the CD-ROM, and access them when you need something different. The package also includes thousands of images and symbols, as well as 3D models—all of which can be utilized to create title screens.

Corel's involvement in video goes beyond these two programs. Several new CD-ROMs add to its lineup of products an extensive stock photo library with beautiful images of just about anything you can imagine. Its web series products give you a mix of options, including font collections, thousands of clip art images, video clips and animation files, sound effects files, backgrounds, plus transitions, and simple wipes, that can be used in video CD-ROM and web productions. The sound effects are especially neat, giving you things like cheering crowds and ticking clocks, little extras that can really enhance your projects. There's also a web designer program to put it all to use.

Another exceptional product is Corel's Stock Music Library, which includes many royalty-free music selections in 21 different styles and categories on several CD-ROMs. You can choose between adult contemporary, Christmas, classical, country and western, industrial, rock, world music, corporate, and more. Each music selection has a 10-second, 30-second, and a full (usually 2-minute) version. The music quality is excellent, with real instruments, not totally synthesized. These are stored as .wav files, so you need to import them into your system. An accompanying book gives good descriptions of each piece, helping you locate the right music for your project. It is an incredible deal, one of the best music investments you'll find anywhere. The disk is compatible with virtually all operation systems: PC and Mac, Windows NT and UNIX.

Adobe Illustrator and Photoshop

Adobe Systems carved its niche in the Mac world, and only in recent years converted its popular Illustrator and Photoshop (Figure A–1) programs for the PC platform. The powerful programs deliver incredible control, with sophisticated tools allowing the print or video professional to do just about anything to an image. The Adobe Illustrator includes Adobe Streamline, which converts images from blocky bitmaps to smooth PostScript language images.

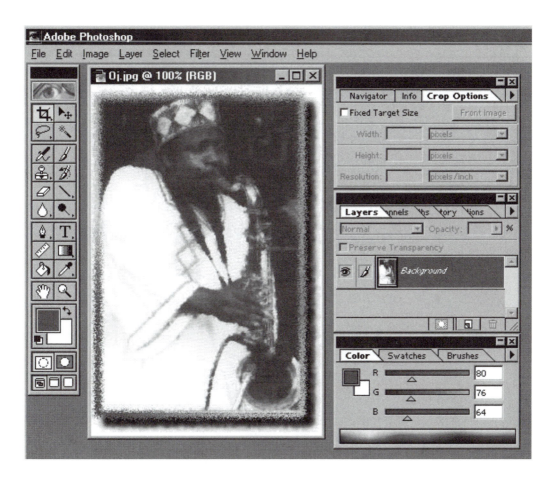

Figure A–1. Adobe Photoshop has long set the standard for painting or pixel-based art programs.

The capability of Adobe products can be overwhelming, providing control the videographer may not require for simple title or logo screens. However, every level of control you master can help you deliver a higher-quality product to customers, ultimately setting you apart from the competition.

Illustrator (vector-based) allows you to enter your text along any path, straight or curved, then edit your composite image with a multitude of tools. You can add thickness, shadows, outlines, and 3D text; blend colors; create transparent type outlines; rotate text; and wrap letters around objects. Be prepared to spend quite a bit of time learning the tools and developing your skills, but Adobe provides an extremely well-documented set of manuals to guide you through the process, from simple exercises to complex procedures.

No computer desktop is complete without a copy of Photoshop, Adobe's stellar painting program. Used by graphics artists throughout the world, each upgrade of its features and capability further establishes it as a leader, the tool most often used for everything from magazine covers to screen icons on TV evening news. When it comes to creating eye-catching title screens for videos and graphics for Internet websites, Photoshop does the job with style.

Photoshop brings to the table a number of functions that make life easier and expand your capability. Many effects that once required additional plug-in software or third party programs now can be done by Photoshop directly. You can add drop shadows, bevels, and glows directly from the Effects menu.

ACTIONS AND REACTIONS

The Actions command allows you to "program" multiple keystroke or mouse-activated commands and operations and assign them to a single key. Pressing the assigned key can activate them. For example, adding a drop shadow ordinarily requires you to go to the Effects menu and select Drop Shadow, a task that takes several moves to complete. Now you can select an object and press the assigned key. Photoshop takes care of the rest.

In addition, Photoshop comes with sets containing more than 100 different preset Actions. You can find them in the Goodies folder inside the Photoshop application folder. For example, several of these Actions will create various types of picture frames around your images. If you like the frame but want to it be a little bit different for your image, you can customize it easily.

Special tools include the Automatic Lasso and Automatic Pen, which will follow or trace along an object's outline. This makes selecting objects and separating them from their backgrounds much, much easier. Parameter adjustments let you set the level of sensitivity for defining edges and anchor points.

ADDING TEXT

The Text tool opens up a text box where you type in words or a title. When you change the text in the box, such as the font or font size, you can see that change updated automatically at the full size on the main project screen. Formatting control includes leading, kerning, and tracking. You can mix font sizes and even font styles within a word or single text box. Text color is another option. You can move and position text on the main screen while the Text dialog box is still open. Simply click outside the box, position the text, then go back to the dialog box for further modifications. Go outside the Text dialog box to apply effects like the bevel or glow to selected text.

Text on its own layer can be modified and edited, even if an effect has been applied.

Simply double-click on the *T* in the text layer of the Layers palette to bring up the Type dialog box and make your modifications. Any effects done previously will be adapted to the changed text so you don't lose work already done. Effects themselves can be modified. Double-clicking on the Effects icon in the Layers menu reopens the Effects dialog box, so you can change its parameters as well: Add more shadow, reduce a bevel, edit until you're satisfied. Text layers are automatically named after the text they contain. Now when you are looking through your Layers palette it is easier to tell which layers contain text.

UNDO/REDO

Early versions of Photoshop had only one level of Undo, insufficient since many actions require several steps to accomplish. The latest release lets you see a visual history of every action performed through the History palette.

It maintains a record of all your keystrokes and mouse moves. You choose the point to which you will return. You can undo one, two, or a dozen steps; drag out one step while leaving the rest; or insert a new step.

MacroMedia Fireworks

Fireworks (Figure A–2) is a program by MacroMedia specifically designed for creating web and Internet graphics. By not trying to be all things for all people, it can eliminate functions that apply only to the print medium, such as CMYK processing. Instead, it can concentrate on elements important to web designers, from .gif animation to JavaScript rollovers. It streamlines web graphic design by incorporating within a single program many elements that previously took several programs to accomplish.

Ordinarily art programs are either vector (line) or bitmap (pixel) based, which means the graphic artist often must shift from one to another

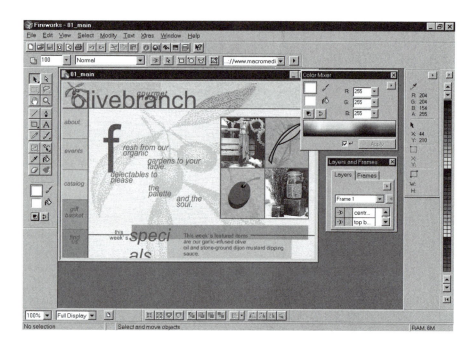

Figure A–2. MacroMedia's Fireworks combines vector and pixel image editing into a single program.

to accomplish the task at hand. Vector software generally is used to create the basic shape and size of an image and a bitmap program to rasterize (convert the vectors to pixels) and apply filters that will generate such things as a shadow or glow. The next step usually is to enter yet another program that optimizes the image for the Web. Fireworks streamlines the process by giving you all of these functions within one program. That it combines vector-style image control with bitmap manipulation is particularly extraordinary.

Opening Fireworks brings up the generally familiar screen layout (Figure A–2), with an icon info bar across the top and a toolbox with 32 tools, some of which are bundled into tool groups. You see common tools like a magnifying glass, lasso, color sampler, pen, and pencil.

When working with websites, pages and even objects will have an individual address identified by their URL (uniform resource locator). Fireworks provides a URL toolbar, which allows you to create URL shapes; select, move, and resize URL objects; and create and edit links—all important functions for website design.

Fireworks' animation truly makes it a full-function tool for the Web. You can work frame by frame or let features such as "looping" to do the work for you. The animation can be previewed in a real-time mode before committing to a finished render. Animation often comprises a single image repeated over and over in many frames. Ordinarily, to make a change in that object, such as changing a border color from blue to red, you have to go to each frame and change every object individually. Fireworks lets you establish the primary object as a "symbol." Repeats of the symbol in subsequent frames are called *instances*. If you make a change in the symbol, that information is passed on along to all instances, updating them automatically. Automatic features like "tweening" can vary elements such as opacity or bevel depth over time.

MacroMedia
600 Townsend
San Francisco, CA 94103

Ulead PhotoImpact

PhotoImpact (Figure A–3) is an art program specifically designed for placing images on the Web. It includes shortcuts and relatively instant options

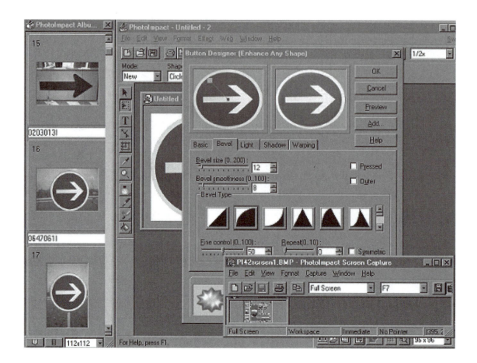

Figure A–3. Ulead's PhotoImpact provides lots of shortcuts for web design.

for creating elements considered desirable for Internet design, such as drop shadows and all kinds of picture frames. You can turn any shape into a 3D button, commonly used for website navigation. Also included is a background designer, for creating seamless color patterns and textures that can add a bit of life to your web page.

All the typical tools and functions are there: zoom control, paint brushes, and layer options. Words or titles can appear in a wide selection of fonts that can be scaled to almost any size, in any color, or with a surface texture. As you add numerous layers to an image, all of them can be revisited and edited. This significantly increases your flexibility on a project.

One of the most important features of PhotoImpact is Smart Saver, which magnifies the compression level of your images by many times. A .jpeg file of 90 MB can be reduced to as small as 10 MB with little or no visible change. Smart Saver gives you a side by side comparison, with a readout of the file size above each image so you can evaluate the before and after versions of Smart Saver's compression. A slide switch allows you to adjust the level of compression so you can control the file size relative to image quality. You also can compare the result of different file types, such as 256-color .gif against full-color .jpeg.

Ulead Systems
970 West 190th Street, Suite 520
Torrance, CA 90502
www.ulead.com

Strata's Media Paint and Special Effects Pack

Although a relatively newer player on the block, Strata hit the ground running, with programs that have been specifically designed for video production (Figure A–4). Some of its strongest attributes are that it works with moving video to create special animated effects and filter layers that permit the editor to modify or enhance a video segment without affecting the original material. As a testament to their quality, you can see Media Paint's effects on several network and syndicated programs, including *Hercules* and *Xena*. Some of the highlights include lightning, fire, and plasma—all with programmable parameters for added realism and originality. You can have a blue lightning bolt streak through the sky, strike a person walking down the road, and explode the person into tiny particles. It's nothing short of amazing.

Strata is the only program listed here or, to my knowledge, available in the consumer or semi-pro arena that allows you to paint over a timeline and not just on a single-frame image. This lets you rotoscope, a popular effect that combines animation with real images, often seen in music videos, where the performer is outlined in a Day-Glo color. The limits of this program are yet to be explored as it comes into the hands of more videographers. While it still functions as a traditional art program, its video compatibility makes it very attractive.

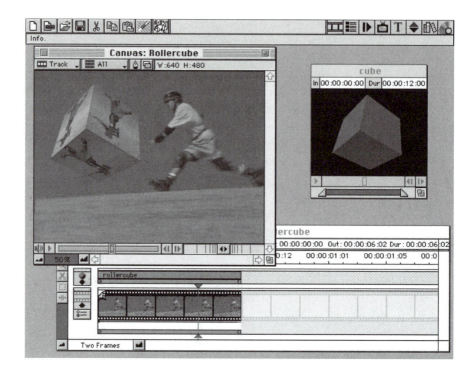

Figure A–4. Strata's Media Paint combines special effects with a typical painting program.

Strata Inc.
2 West St. George Blvd.
St. George, UT 84770
801-629-5218
www.strata3d.com

BUY-OUT ANIMATION AND BACKGROUNDS

Nova Development Corporation's Web Explosion 20,000 and Web Animation Explosion

To brighten your website you need colorful graphics. If you design websites for friends, family, or as a business, then a vast library of fast-loading, attractive graphics and animation is a godsend. Web Explosion 20,000 and Web Animation Explosion are just two of the many clip art and other copyright-free libraries brought to you by Nova Development Corp. These two collections, specifically gathered for use on the Internet, will speed your efforts while giving you movement and sweet eye candy galore. Web Explosion fills you with 10,000 buttons, 250 different banners, 500 bullets, 1,000 separators, 750 repeating background tiles, 7,000 clip art images, 1,000 photos, and more—eye-popping neon art, retro, classic marble and granite textures—all ready to place on your web page.

Animation Explosion gives you dozens of animated buttons and banners, plus cartoons, 3D animation, and over 250 pieces of interactive Shockwave animation. You have what seems like an infinite number of different categories to choose from, something for any occasion or application. As an added bonus, you receive a copy of Ulead's .gif animator, so you can make your own animation using the images on the CD-ROM. Nova makes it easy and fun, the fast way to add a splash of color and movement to your website.

Nova Development Corporation
23801 Calabasas Road, Suite 2005
Calabasas, CA 91302
818-591-9600
http://www.novadevcorp.com

SPECIAL EFFECTS AND TRANSITIONS

Adobe After Effects

Adobe's After Effects creates animation with an unlimited layering of video elements to produce eye candy that boggles the mind. It is used regularly for the openers of TV shows, which have many different images fading in and out and moving across the screen simultaneously. Animation properties can be applied to full-motion video as well as still objects, with a system that is fairly easy to understand and operate. Adobe purposely designed After Effects so that it could work with its other software, including Illustrator and its editing system Premier, giving most users a jump start on using the program.

After Effects uses a timeline, during which various video elements appear or disappear, move, or are affected in some way. Keyframes target when and where an event will take place. The editor applies any of a number of properties to the screen elements to create the desired look or effect.

The easiest way to add motion is to have your objects follow a path. This can be as simple as drawing a path on the screen and having an object follow it. Elements of the program can take your rough freehand (or mouse-drawn) path and smooth it into gentle curves that are more appropriate and pleasant to view. You can preview your object's motion through a wireframe model. This gives you the basic idea of how your animation will look without going through any extensive rendering.

Unique to After Effects is its separate control over time and motion. In real life, objects can have varying velocities, accelerating as they gain momentum or decelerating as they come to a stop. Many animation programs are strictly linear or can apply only a single speed. The ability to vary and adjust motion speed gives animation an added realism that directly affects audience perception. Acceleration and deceleration even can be combined along a motion path, such as if an object were going up and down hills.

After Effects chroma key control is a strong addition to the package. It offers many subtle ways to extract the best performance from your keyed video, giving you layered video with clean edges, suppressing color spillover, even letting you cut out undesirable elements that aren't removed through the normal keying process.

An especially nice quality of After Effects is its open architecture design, which means that third party developers can create plug-in programs that enhance and expand the program's capabilities. This can range from additional filters to specific effects, giving you more variety and ways to make your video stand out.

Boris Effects

Boris Effects is a software plug-in designed for use with a variety of computer editing systems, including Avid MCXpress, FAST Video Machine, Adobe Premiere, and Adobe After Effects. The program is easy to learn, and once you have the basics down, you can develop custom effects and transitions. Boris Effects's prepackaged transitions probably will take care of your requirements for a long time to come, but for those times when only something unique will do, the tools are there for you to use.

For the quick and easy approach, locate the keyframe library, which gives you a huge array of preprogrammed effects from page turns to PIP. A new Windows screen appears giving you a variety of subheadings, including things like tumble and spin or a variety of pushes, fancy dissolves and wipes, video split effects, plus cubes and slabs. In the files under each heading 20 or more variations on a similar theme. Simply click on one of them and you return to the Boris Main screen with your selection loaded. Boris Effects gives you support for an unlimited number of video tracks to create multi-window effects rivaling the big networks. Boris FX also is your source for filters, including color correction and Color FX. The new Curvilinear FX filters add a ripple, bulge, wave, and more.

You can directly control virtually every effect parameter, including distance or depth, position, and speed and acceleration. All effects have a duration, that is, they take place on a timeline. At specified points along the timeline, the Keyframes, various parameters may be set or changed.

Another thing you get with Boris Effects is an excellent chrominance and luminance keyer. The chroma keying I have seen on other systems can leave a lot to be desired, with a lot of noise at the edge of the keyed image, but Boris Effects has created a winner. Edges are clean, without the blue halo that sometimes gets left behind. The chroma key also works with a fairly wide range of color, so even if your lighting on the background color is not perfect you can still get a good clean key.

Boris Effects has a couple of different options for helping you work faster, always a consideration in nonlinear editing. First, you can select a faster preview mode. This disables the antialiasing that keeps images looking smooth. The same logic can be extended to the actual rendering of the effect. Rendering complex effects can be quite time consuming and you may be disappointed if, after 5 or 10 minutes of rendering, the effect isn't to your liking for one reason or another. Boris Effects allows you to use a "draft render" mode that disables the antialiasing, greatly reducing the rendering time. Later, when your editing is complete and you are fully satisfied with the results, you can rerender the effects, letting the computer do its work while you do something else.

Artel Software
374 Congress Street, Suite 308
Boston, Massachusetts 02210
http://www.artelsoft.com
http://www.borisfx.com

Video SpiceRack

The cleverly named Video SpiceRack effects collection (Figure A–5) differs from other systems in that it is not a plug-in per se. This impressive collection of mattes and transitions is not installed as a program into your computer at all. Rather, it is a catalog that can either be copied to your hard drive or accessed directly from the CD-ROM.

With several hundred effects included in the package, something is there for most every purpose. The effects are organized into visually distinct categories: CoolWipes, Pure and Simple, Organix, WonderBands, and Standards Plus. These are further subdivided for easy identification with descriptive titles like Kaleidos, LiveWipes, Textures, Videogami, and IrisEssentials.

Included in the catalog are several identical sets of gradient image files, each set configured for use in one of many different output require-

Figure A–5. Video SpiceRack uses gradient matte overlays to create an infinite variety of transitions (see color insert).

ments, such as quarter-screen, NTSC, Targa NTSC, PAL, or CCIR-601. This is necessary since it is important for the gradient image to match the frame size of your final output for the cleanest result.

Each effect can be customized to add even greater diversity and used in a variety of applications, from transitions to matte screens, or to form unique split screens. This customization process can be accomplished on any image editing application, since the effect in reality is a gradient, not a process.

Perhaps the most attractive quality of the collection is the almost ethereal elegance so many of the effects convey. One reason for this visual elegance is the soft-edged quality that is a prime feature of the SpiceRack catalog. The degree of soft edge can be extensively edited, but the concept of the gradient image imparts this quality within the inherent design. This makes even the patterned and fragmented selections seem somehow organic, rather than a digital manipulation. Pixelan Software describes this as supersoftening, and it provides you with a level of subtlety that dramatically alters your video content.

SpiceRack can be used with a variety of Windows-based editing systems, including Adobe Premiere (4.0 or later) and After Effects (3.0 or later), and the Windows-based programs Discreet Logic D-Vision (3.5 or later), FAST Video Machine (all except the lite versions), in:sync Speed Razor (all versions), and Pinnacle Studio 400. In fact users of Adobe Premier with the Pinnacle ReelTime and Blossom Fury nonlinear editors already may be familiar with the SpiceRack concept through a version of SpiceRack Lite that comes bundled with those systems. We are told compatibility with other nonlinear systems is on the way.

Inscriber Character Generator

One of the most popular character generators was developed by Inscriber Technology and is incorporated into many of today's nonlinear editing systems (Figure A–6). However the standard plug-in of Inscriber could be called Inscriber Lite, and a full-blown version, Inscriber FeaturePak, can be operated as an advanced plug-in or stand-alone program. It offers some of the best looking antialiased fonts you will ever see, with a range of controls that give you really great looking titles.

The system comes with some 250 basic fonts and you can add True Type fonts for more selection and variations than you can even imagine.

Figure A–6. Inscriber Technology is well established as the premier character generator for professional-level nonlinear editing.

Type in (or click on up/down arrows) all the characteristics of your type-face: size, slant, kerning, width, and more. All fonts are scaleable from 10 to 999 points. Add any amount of italic slant you want one digit at a time. Increase the width without changing the height.

The menu also gives you access to the shadow and edge attributes. Select a standard drop shadow, an offset, or an extruded look. Pick any direction for the shadow at the click of a mouse button. Your typeface edges can be defined for thickness and style, including outline, embossing, or glow.

Another feature is "rotation" control. Here you can set your titles at an infinitely variable angle, adjustable either by typing in the rotation box directly, clicking on the up/down arrows next to the box, or grabbing your title in the workspace and manually placing it at the desired angle. You don't need to exit your editing program to create these angles in your painting or drawing program, you do it directly in your editor. This is a great feature, breaking up the static horizontal title lines with another variation of two dimensions. It is one of the looks that separates higher-end productions from those done on amateur equipment.

The color and texture tabs allow you to define the appearance of your letters, boxes, or frames. You can select separate colors for the main body of the text, the shadow, and the edge; in fact you can do a two-color blend for any one of these elements. Blends can be slanted at any angle, adding to the variety and eye appeal. Select colors from a variety of palettes or use the eye dropper icon to sample color from anywhere on the screen. Textures such as marble or wood grain can be easily imported and applied. In this menu you also can define the transparency level for each element of the title: foreground, edge, and shadow. Along with transparency adjustments to the entire element, you can alter the density of the top relative to the bottom. In other words, letters or a drawn screen element can fade out at the top or bottom.

You can treat letters individually or apply changes to the entire group at once: Choose the Styles tab and assign a specified style (or create a new style) to your group of letters. As you change one line of your text, those changes also are made to other lines. Or the letters and words can be different sizes and colors, within one line or among different lines.

Titles and boxes seem to go together and Inscriber provides a quick, easy way for you to create them. Once you are in the graphic object portion of the program, click and drag to create a box of any size. Select one of the format options to instantly add beveled edges, rounded corners, or choose other shapes such as an oval. Again, make your box and its edges any color or a two-toned blend of colors. You have the same variety of options for colors and transparency levels. Beveled options automatically blend colors to add sheen and dimension.

The template option can make your work much faster and simpler by providing a variety of design parameters that can be applied at the click of a mouse. You can use existing templates or create your own, which then are available for any future project.

MotionPak is a software upgrade to Inscriber that enables the titles to fly about the screen. The animation program works by allowing you to define key frame positions and motion paths. A wire frame preview mode gives you fast feedback to see exactly how the animation will look before it is rendered. Placement, Shape, and Filter tabs give you the ability to change how the object appears over time. You also can control the timing along the path as well as affect the smoothness of travel for more fluid movement. Another option is to skip the custom control and opt for the preset motion templates, a quick and easy way to get to standard moves and motions.

Inscriber Technology Corporation
180 King Street South, 3rd Floor
Waterloo, Ontario, Canada N2J 1P8
800-363-3400 or 519-570-9111; fax 519-570-9111
www.inscriber.com

MUSIC AND AUDIO SOFTWARE

Sonic Desktop SmartSound

The computer solution for music at your fingertips can be found in the Sonic Desktop SmartSound software. This unique program uses pre-recorded music phrases that can be combined in a multitude of ways to put together beautiful copyright-free music.

You can create your music by selecting one of several directions or options. Choose a style, like rock, country, or classical. Decide on a length, 10, 30, 60 seconds, or longer. After you've narrowed your choices to a particular basic melody, SmartSound gives you a number of variations on the same tune or theme. One might feature a keyboard lead break, another electric guitar. Go for a dramatic intro or a thunderous close. Once you find the one that works best for your application, save it as a .wav file, which can be imported into your computer video editing program.

You can go one step further by creating your own arrangements on an audio timeline, much the way you work with video in a nonlinear editing program. SmartSound offers a library of musical phrases, four-bar patterns with all instruments, and a variety of openers, endings, and melodies and transitions—all the pieces the program uses when it does the work for you. Here you make your own choices, arranging the sections to suit you and your production. Simply drag and drop the segment blocks along the time-line, inserting or deleting as necessary. Then play back your composition for an instant review.

Again, this is not a bunch of electronically generated music that sounds like it came from a computer but real instruments that give the selections an impressive sound. It's a fun way to come up with music that always fits your video in every way.

Sound Forge

Sound Forge was made for both the digital audio technician and the video editor. The Sound Forge interface is easy to set up and to use: intuitive, log-ically organized, and constructed for use by beginners as well as pros. The program provides two tracks of audio for recording and processing, visually represented on the main screen with the familiar audio waveform display. Audio tracks can be mixed together to create new material and other inter-esting effects. The standard format is the familiar .wav file, but a multitude of other formats are recognized and accessed. Sound files can be either 8 or 16 bit, and sampling rates range from 2,000 Hz to 60,000 Hz. Standard edit-ing and recording is a remarkably straightforward process, with visual win-dows giving you indications of level control and other information regarding your activities.

Three basic menu systems hold the processing tools: Process, Effects, and Tools. The number of options available is truly impressive. Once an effect is accessed, an array of additional tools can fine-tune the effect, giving you enormous creative control. Chances are, you won't use all of these tools and effects, but it's exhilarating just to know they're available. Consider this partial list: three types of EQ (audio equalization or tone control), Graphic, Paragraphic, and Parametric; Fade In and Fade Out; Invert/Flip; Mute; Pan; Reverse; Smooth/Enhance; Compress/Expand Time; four-band dynamic compressor/limiter.

Editing your sound files is not unlike working with a word processor. Cut, Copy, Paste, Overwrite, Trim, Preview, and more are available with the standard Windows icons. Add to this a great variety of detailed sound-shaping tools, such as Chorus, Delay, Distortion, Pitch, Flange/Wah-Wah, Reverb, and Vibrato. Adding reverberation, or really any other effect, is equally simple. Make your selection, which can be the entire file or any portion of it, and choose the alterations you want. As you choose, you have the option to preview your selection either on command or automatically.

Sound Forge also provides Video for Windows (.avi) file support, which enables you to edit your audio tracks while viewing video frames from your production. The .avi files open directly into Sound Forge and display exact video framing above the corresponding waveform. This means that you need not guess about your synchronization to video, maintaining critical timing of images to audio.

The audio timeline itself is calibrated with a time ruler located above the waveform display, and a level ruler on the left side helps you to estimate values in percentage or decibels. This graphic representation conforms to familiar screen displays for nonlinear video editing systems. Other qualities that make digital video editing so convenient are present in the Sound Forge audio system, such as multilevel Undo and Redo, Drag and Drop, multiple windows, and more. All of these elements make Sound Forge familiar and intuitive for anyone already working in the PC/Windows environment.

Band-in-a-Box

Band-in-a-Box, by PG Music, makes it easy for you to put together your own music, original songs and compositions, with minimal musical background or knowledge. While you don't need to know how to read music or even keep a beat, you should have some idea of basic chord progressions and what notes or keys work together. It basically works like this. First you enter in the chord pattern using their whole note names, like A, D, or E. Then you select a style, and there are literally dozens to chose from, with several variations on each: rock, country, blues, reggae, jazz—and each has its own interpretation and theme. Tell Band-in-a-Box to play back your composition, and it will add drums, bass, keyboard, guitar, and more. It's a great way to try out sample melodies and put together songs.

PG Music, Band-in-a-Box
11-266 Elmwood Avenue
Buffalo, NY 14222

250-475-2874 or 800-268-6272
http://www.pgmusic.com

PowerTracks

The companion sequence program to Band-in-a-Box is PowerTracks, also by
PG Music. Songs created in Band-in-a-Box can be saved as MIDI files and
imported into PowerTracks (or any other similar MIDI sequencer), where
they can then be modified in any number of ways. PowerTracks will display
each instrument on its own track, giving you multitrack audio capability.
You modify each track individually by adding, erasing, or changing notes or
play an entirely new arrangement using a MIDI instrument keyboard. You
can dump the Band-in-a-Box bass line and insert your own.

PowerTracks is intuitive, easy to work with, and incredibly affordable.
It contains most of the important elements of a professional sequencer,
working essentially like a word processor except with musical elements. Cut
and Paste, Delete, Insert, Move—all in single measures or whole blocks of
time, single or multiple tracks.

PG Music, Band-in-a-Box
11-266 Elmwood Avenue
Buffalo, NY 14222
250-475-2874 or 800-268-6272
http://www.pgmusic.com

Cakewalk

Cakewalk is a music sequencer that gives you up to 256 separate MIDI-
compatible audio tracks. It also is a digital audio recorder, meaning you can
record live audio right on to your computer's hard drive. In addition to the
MIDI tracks imported from a disk or generated by a music keyboard, you
can connect a microphone and record vocals or other instruments to individual tracks. Add electric guitar, maracas, or go the route of sound effects,
enhancing natural sound with more dramatic audio just as they do in Holly-
wood. The only limitation is the available space on your hard drive.

Cakewalk also gives you the ability to add digital audio effects.
Enhance your audio tracks with Reverb, Chorus, and Delay. The addition of

computer-generated effects within the program is really a plus, putting the entire recording toolkit in your hands.

Cakewalk
5 Cambridge Center
Cambridge, MA 02142
800-234-1171; fax 800-370-6912
http://www.cakewalk.com

SoundTrek's Jammer

Jammer, by SoundTrek, in a way combines the features of Band-in-a-Box and a sequencer. Jammer gives you a 256-track sequencer with full MIDI recording, compositing, and mixing, but that's just the beginning. Jammer is a songwriter's tool, providing over 200 assorted intros, grooves, breaks, and endings that can be mixed to help you develop your songs. Create original chord progressions, then add up to five-part harmony to your melody.

Click the mouse, and Jammer puts together the accompaniment of a full band, with bass and drums, horns and keyboards. Want to hear a different variation of the theme? Click on Compose. Instantly Jammer puts together new parts, with millions of possibilities. All songs can be edited using typical tools and commands like Copy and Paste or Drag and Drop, making it quick and easy to customize Jammer tunes with your own arrangements and ideas.

SoundTrek, Jammer
3408 Howell Street, Suite F
Duluth, GA 30136
770-623-1338
www.soundtrek.com

Virtual Sound Canvas

One the biggest names in electronic musical instruments is Roland. Roland's Virtual Sound Canvas directs MIDI file data through the Pentium CPU rather than your sound card, enhancing and improving your sound to that of a full-fledged MIDI/GS format synthesizer. It gives computer users superior performance over inexpensive audio cards, and instant access to a selection of instrumentation, things like drums, bass, piano sounds, over

200 total. As a system it is capable of playing dozens of sounds simultaneously (128 polyphony), with audio effects like reverberation (echo), chorus, 16-bit stereo, sampled at 22.05 KHz.

The Virtual Sound Canvas music pack is centered around the Sound Canvas, the tools you need to start playing with MIDI. First you get 100 royalty free MIDI files, music ready to go. Easy Juke 2 is a program you can use to keep your sound files organized. It also will play back MIDI sequences you purchase, both licensed, well-known songs, and copyright-free tunes.

SOURCES FOR COPYRIGHT-FREE MUSIC

PBTM
1350 Chambers
Eugene, OR 97402
541-345-0212
http:/www.PBTM.com

Energetic Music
P.O. Box 84583
Seattle, WA 98124
800-323-2972
Demo 206-467-6931

The Ultimate Music Collection CD-ROM
Canary Productions
P.O. Box 202
Bryn Mawr, PA 19010
888-4CANARY (888-422-6279) or 610-971-9490; fax 610-971-9630

WEB PAGE DESIGN AND INTERNET VIDEO PUBLISHING SOFTWARE

MacroMedia's DreamWeaver

DreamWeaver, by MacroMedia, is hailed as one of the best web editors on the market today, simple enough for the beginner to use and understand yet with all the complex bells and whistles a pro developer might want.

Those who know say DreamWeaver writes clean code or HTML, the programming language behind everything we see and hear on the Web. Unlike other web editing programs, which throw in proprietary programming language amidst their HTML, DreamWeaver gets the job done pure and simple. This can be especially important if you work with several editing programs, allowing you to import files from one program to another.

MacroMedia
600 Townsend
San Francisco, CA 94103

Real Networks' RealProducer Plus

One of the most popular programs for streaming video and audio, RealProducer Plus by Real Networks, is a plug-in that the end user downloads into his or her computer. RealPlayer Plus has been considered the third most popular download on the Internet, with over 43 million downloads from the site, www.real.com, one of the 20 most-visited sites on the Web. It has been estimated that up to 85% of all sites with streaming media may use RealAudio, RealVideo, or RealFlash, Real Networks' software for streaming animation. More than 150,000 hours of live content using RealAudio and RealVideo are produced every week. Over 1000 radio stations broadcast live on the Web using RealAudio and 30 TV stations air programming using RealVideo.

How do you turn your video into a RealVideo movie? RealProducer Plus converts audio .wav files and video .avi and .mov files into RealAudio and RealVideo files. These files are linked to your website, in more or less the same way as .jpeg and .gif images, residing on your server. Part of your page design sends out a call for RealPlayer Plus. Surfers at your site with RealPlayer Plus already on their computers will be ready to go, otherwise they can be directed to the RealPlayer Plus website for a download. Another option is to embed the RealPlayer Plus software into your web page.

RealProducer Plus makes it easy to convert video and audio files, using the Wizard mode, which guides you step by step through the process. Begin a New Session, then select the file you want to convert. Next a screen pops up that lets you enter the Title, Author, and copyright information for your clip, which can be displayed when someone explores your site, useful, for example, if you are selling music CDs and using RealAudio. You can specify your Target Audience, decide what connection speed most of your audience will have. You also can select the level of video quality. Click Finish, and RealProducer Plus does the rest. Check your recording by clicking on Play. If everything is as you like it, you can ready post it on the Web.

RealProducer Plus uses the same type of Wizard walk through to help you turn your files into HTML, ready for the Web. Choose either to have a Pop-Up Player, which directs those without RealPlayer Plus to the necessary download, or embed RealPlayer Plus into your site for immediate playback on any system. Decide whether you want the RealAudio or RealVideo file to play back automatically or for the end user to use VCR-type control buttons for playback Start and Stop.

One slight complication is that RealPlayer Plus has been through several generations of evolution, and with each improvement, it becomes necessary to upgrade the publishing program and for the end viewers to upgrade their player software. It's a constant game of leapfrog, which is part of the technology growth curve.

Geo-Interactive Media Group's Web Charger

Web Charger, by the Geo-Interactive Media Group, exists for one reason: streamlining web images for lightning fast downloading. Using a proprietary compression scheme, Web Charger reduces file sizes by up to 400% more than the standard .jpeg, yet its images can be downloaded and displayed by any .jpeg-compatible Internet browser.

You begin by selecting the bandwidth for the image you wish to compress; that is, the modem speed and its ability to transfer information into the end user's computer. Typically 28.8 modems can transfer data at 3.5 KB per second, provided the web connection is operating at proper efficiency. This means a 7-KB image should download in 2 seconds. If you know the person on the receiving end is connected to the Internet via a high-speed ISDN line capable of transferring 8 KB per second, Web Charger can reduce the compression or the picture will simply download that much faster.

Next open or import your photo or image into the Web Charger workspace. From here you have a variety of options. You can define the compression parameters, deciding to compress your image by defining the file size, the download time, or image quality. Assign your choice the highest priority, and the other two parameters will be adjusted automatically. Do you want maximum image quality or are you willing to settle for something like

70% of the original? Often to the eye there is little or no visible change. If you are shooting for a 2-second download time, Web Charger can compress the file with that in mind, basing compression on image dimensions and file size.

Web Charger takes preservation of image quality one step further, by allowing you to define certain areas of the image to preserve image quality while allowing less critical areas to achieve maximum compression. Various selection tools, such as a square, an ellipse, or a custom shape tool, allow you to define areas and determine how much compression to apply. Often background portions are of little importance and a loss of image quality can pass almost unnoticed. By preserving the resolution of the main subject, you ensure the quality of your image while maximizing the compression potential.

Web Charger allows you to compare the original with the compressed image, so you can make modifications as necessary, increasing or reducing compression to suit your preference. Often a fast-loading site is the edge you need to hold web surfers' interests, encouraging them to explore deeper. Web Charger can make the difference, allowing you to maintain compelling visuals without compromising download times.

Geo-Interactive Media Group's VideoPro

VideoPro (Figure A–7), also by the Geo-Interactive Media Group, makes it possible for anyone with a computer and a modest budget to place video and audio that you can see and hear on the Internet using almost any current Internet browser. VideoPro works with any standard .avi file, the format for video used by PC-compatible computers.

Once you decide which modem speed to target, you can select a compression setting. Fortunately Geo already has determined which compression settings work best at specific bandwidths, and several preset choices are available. If you are working with a number of video clips, they can be batch processed, compressed all at once, saving you time and effort.

Another choice is the amount of buffer space required. Basically you decide how much information the VideoPro player should download before playback actually begins. This can help ensure that your "movie" plays smoothly and uninterruptedly.

Once your .avi is processed, it is saved to a folder with several other files, Emblaze proprietary JavaScripts. You also must place within the folder

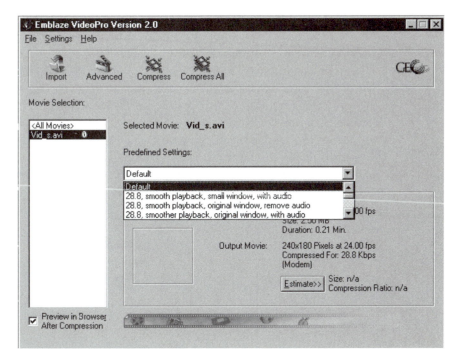

Figure A–7. VideoPro enables you to add video to a website without requiring visitors to download a media player.

the Emblaze Video Player files, which are available from a folder within the program or on the program's CD-ROM. When uploading the video to your website, all these files must be present for the video to function, especially the player files. This player is what enables end users to see your video without a plug-in.

Emblaze Hot Spots

The purpose of Emblaze Hot Spots is to enhance your website through interactive areas on the screen, similar to what one might expect from a CD-ROM. Emblaze Hot Spots takes your hot spots to the next level to generate rollovers, actions initiated by a mouse that lets the person viewing your page know a link exists. As you pass over a hot link, the image underneath changes, giving the person browsing a visual indication that a link is present. Emblaze Hot Spots automates this process with a process that is effortless to follow and understand.

The program is unbelievably easy to use, very straightforward at accomplishing its mission. If you want to change the way an image looks, the before and after states are created first in a graphics program. The first, before, state is loaded into the Emblaze Hot Spots work space as the background, then a hot spot area is defined by drawing around the area's shape. Next you define the action.

A new screen will appear with various options. You enter the proper information such as, "When the mouse rolls over the hot spot, insert this image"(choose your image from a library of images imported earlier or import one then and place it in the library) or "When the mouse rolls over the hot spot play this sound" (select a sound from the library provided). The sound library contains clicks of various kinds, beeps, boings, water droplets, plus nature sounds and musical notes. You can create your own sounds and import them.

The second state defines the actions when the mouse actually is clicked on the hot spot. Again it can be another image, a different sound, or a different shape to the cursor. When finished, preview the action within the program to decide if it works properly and you are satisfied with all the elements.

Save the work as a special Emblaze file, which can be reopened and edited at a later date, or export it ready for action on a web page. Emblaze Hot Spots creates all the necessary HTML, as well as the other JavaScripting and custom files to make the whole thing work, then places them in a folder that you name and place on your hard drive. Incorporate the hot spot into a web page, check it once again with your Internet browser, and you're ready to upload it to your website.

VIDEO CARD

Truevision Targa RTX Video Card

In semi-technical terms, the heart of the Targa RTX board is the dual set of LSI-codec .jpeg processors from LSI Logic. These decompress the video from a hard drive. The original Targa 2000 cards and the current 1000 cards have only one codec. With two, the RTX board simultaneously can process two streams, essentially two layers of video. The video is placed in a V RAM buffer, where the system architecture can process the 2D effects in faster than real time, which allows them to be displayed on your computer screen or monitor in true real time.

The Targa 2000 RTX board offers one very significant improvement over the earlier Targa 2000, something it calls a *breakout box*. The breakout box, which can be either rack mounted or placed on the desktop, gives the end user a more convenient, easy way to make video and audio connections, accepting composite, S-Video, or Component video used with the Betacam SP format. The older Targa 2000 simply had a 4-foot cable, which plugged into the Targa board on one end and had a bunch of loose cables and connectors at the other. The breakout box, particularly if it is rack mounted, provides a solid, stable connection interface, allowing the editor to change out decks and other video and audio sources at will.

Another feature worthy of mention involves the audio connections. Unlike the original 2000, which provided only unbalanced male RCA connectors, the RTX board gives you balanced input/output audio connections. RCA style connectors are provided as well, so any video or audio device can be plugged in quickly and easily. There also is a hook up for an alpha channel connection as well as a provision for a genlock signal.

Glossary

Every hobby or line of work has its own special words, jargon you won't find in the dictionary but that has very real meaning in the world where it is used. Desktop video is no exception, in fact it has an overabundance of words with a special connotation when used in reference to video or exist only to describe a specific function, an anomaly. At the same time new words are added or created with every changing development in digital video technology. One could probably write a dictionary of nothing but terms for video production. We tried to cover the most important and common words you're likely to run across. If you are new to computers, video, or video production, pay special attention here. Before you know it, you'll be spewing acronyms and dropping buzz words with the best, able to spot a glitch, create an EDL, or assemble an A/B roll.

A/B roll.   A/B roll comes from the world of linear editing and tape. A and B represent two source or playback VCRs, each with a scene that will be recorded to the edit master videotape. A video mixer of some type is used to make the transition from one video segment to another. Both tapes "roll" or play simultaneously, and at a specific point during the editing, a transition takes place going from source tape A to source tape B. Computer nonlinear editing has made this way of creating a transition almost a thing of the past.

Animation.   Digitally created frames that give the appearance of full-motion video when played back in rapid succession. Animation created by the digital desktop video systems are used in all forms of video production, from websites to broadcast television. Dedicated software is available to automate many elements of the process.

Array.   A series of several hard disk drives electronically linked for maximum storage capacity. Drives may be partitioned to operate independently or "striped" so that they appear to your editing software as one drive.

Applet. A type of JavaScript for the Internet, used for fast loading, complex animation.

.avi. A file format for PC computers for display or playback of both video and audio within a single file.

Batch capture. The computer is used to control a videotape source (camcorder or VCR), automatically recording or digitizing selected video and audio scenes to the hard drive.

B roll. Video images specifically shot or recorded to be used as accents in a finished production, complementing the primary or A video. Also known as cutaway, these shots are used to bridge a change in camera angle, camera position, or in place of a transition. (*See also* Cutaways.)

Breakout box. An interface from your video card to the Input and Output connections for video and audio equipment. Instead of making all connections directly on the card itself from the back of the computer, the breakout box provides a convenient hook-up for all relevant devices. It can be installed on the desktop or rack mounted with other gear.

Chroma key. *Chroma* refers to color. Typically an actor or an object is videoed against a solid color background, usually blue or green. The chroma key system turns the areas of blue or green transparent, leaving only the actor or object. This video is layered or combined with another video source, making the two into one. For example, an actor standing before a blue screen can be placed in front of a new background.

Control L. An interface found on camcorders and VCRs, used for remote control of playback and record functions. The Control L connector uses a mini-phono jack.

Crawl. Graphics or words that move horizontally across the bottom of the TV screen. A common use for a crawl is to display storm warnings or stock reports.

Cutaway. A shot that relates to or contributes information to the main elements of a scene. When shooting on location, the camera operator should look for additional shots that will complement the main production. During editing these shots can be used as extra filler or to cover poor camera moves. For example, an actor is supposed to appear nervous while talking to another person in the scene. The cutaway shot shows a closeup of the actor's hands shaking, reinforcing our perception of nervousness.

Digitize.   Record video and audio into the computer, where it is stored on the computer's hard drive.

Dissolve.   Probably the most common transition you see in video production, in a dissolve, as one segment of video seems to disappear or fade from view another fades into view taking its place. Dissolves range from the "soft cut," which lasts less than a second, to the long dissolve, which may take 2 seconds or more to go from one image to the next.

Dot crawl.   NTSC video uses an interlaced display technique that beams horizontal lines across the TV screen in alternating rows. Areas of the picture with narrow lines, one or two pixels in width, reveal the interlace scan to the eye through the illusion of crawling dots caused by pixels alternating from one scan line to the adjacent line above or below it.

Dropout.   A dropout is a blemish, visible during video playback, that results from an imperfection on the videotape. It can be caused by a speck of dust on the surface of the tape, blocking that part of the tape's recorded information from the playback video heads, or from a defect in the tape itself. A videotape consists of a plastic ribbon coated with an oxide or some other magnetic material. This material can be dislodged from the tape backing, which translates into black specks and streaky lines in a video.

Dub.   Dub commonly refers to making videotape copies (running dubs), whether a single copy or multiple copies for distribution.

Dub master.   A copy of an edited master videotape. Once a video has been edited into a finished program, the next step is to make copies of the program to distribute to family and friends or sell to customers. However, with every playing of the edit master comes wear and tear and even the possibility the tape could be damaged (ever had a VCR eat one of your tapes?). Therefore the wise make a copy of the original master, a dub master, to use when making copies. When the dub master starts to show wear it is discarded and a new copy is made from the original.

DVC (digital video cassette).   A videotape format that records both video and audio as digital signals.

Edit controller.   A device that takes over the playback and record functions of a VCR or camcorder. In linear editing, the edit controller typically takes over operation of two VCRs, camcorders, or any combination of the two. One unit functions as the player, the other as the recorder. The edit controller operates both at once, automating the linear editing process. When the computer functions as the edit controller, it operates the VCR playback for digitizing video clips or producing a video signal from the computer and recording it on videotape.

Edit master.   A videotape consisting of material selected from master tapes, arranged in the order decided on by the editor or person doing the editing; usually considered a finished program.

EDL (edit decision list).   Created from the tape "log" or a nonlinear editing system's video clip library, the EDL is a list of the scenes selected or used to create a finished production. The EDL can be printed in hard copy form or saved on disk and transferred to a compatible nonlinear editing system housed in a separate computer. Often editors will use one system to create an "off-line" or preliminary version and an EDL for an edited production, then use the EDL in a more sophisticated system to generate a higher-resolution "on-line" edit.

Fast and wide media drives.   Because video is so demanding in the speed with which information must be retrieved for real-time playback, special hard drives are required that can transfer bits and bytes at a high rate of speed. Special disk controllers are used to assist in the drives in the rapid assimilation of the video data.

Field.   Every frame of video is composed of two alternating fields, interlaced by your television. NTSC video consists of 30 frames (60 fields) per second of playback.

Frame.   A single complete unit of video, with 30 frames per second of video playback; also a single page on an Internet website. Often a web page consists of several frames combined into a frameset.

Frame capture.   The act of digitizing a single frame of video to a computer's hard drive.

Frame rate.   Standard NTSC video consists of 30 frames per second of playback. Multimedia such as CD-ROMs or Internet video typically reduce file size by changing the frame rate; that is, limiting the number of frames to 8–15 per second.

Gain.   Amplification of an audio or video signal. Many camcorders today allow manually amplifying or adding gain to the video signal, thus boosting the sensitivity in low light.

Generation.   The number of dubs (copies) away from the master tape. The master represents the first generation. The edit master is the second generation. The dub master is the third generation. Dub copies from the dub master are the fourth generation.

.gif. Also known as the Compuserve .gif, this file format was developed as a way to create small graphic files specifically for use on the Internet. Images have a limited palette of only 256 colors, best suited for cartoons and titles.

Glitch. An undesirable element. On your video screen, a glitch can appear as a blemish that blips by during playback or a jerk in the motion cause by a minor technical problem such as an unstable sync pulse from a video source. On a computer a glitch can be a problem within a program that prevents it from working properly.

Graphics. Generally titles and other two-dimensional images (graphs and bar charts, icons, pictures) placed over a video source.

Hard drive array. Certain computer applications, such as editing lengthy video productions, require vast amounts of hard drive space. Manufacturers have responded by assembling cases and other associated hardware that will accommodate multiple drives in a single housing. Software allows the drives to be configured to function as a single large drive or partitioned so that each unit operates and is accessed independently.

Insert edit. With linear editing an insert edit allows adding new video over previously recorded video without disturbing the videotape control track.

Java. A type of scripting for the Internet; a cross-platform language for animation and other applications.

.jpeg. An image file format that employs a compression scheme to radically reduce file size. Images can consist of a 16-million (true) color palette, however, the compression algorithms calculate the removal of redundant pixels when saving or creating the .jpeg file. The primary use is to display full-color images on the Internet.

Key. A special effect that allows one layer of video to be superimposed and merged with another, based on making either a solid color (chroma key) or an area of contrast (luminance) transparent. Chroma and luminance effects are common in many of today's nonlinear editing and computer-based special effects systems.

LANC. Also known as *control L*, it is the edit control interface used by camcorders as well as various consumer and some industrial VCRs. Using a mini-phono plug and jack, the interface permits remote operation of playback and record functions in compatible equipment.

Linear editing.   Tape to tape editing. Video material on master tapes are recorded to another tape, the edit master, one scene after another in linear order.

Lithium batteries.   Replacing nicad-powered batteries, lithium-based batteries eliminate the nicad "memory" effect, charging to full power every time despite the amount of discharge. Other features possible from lithium battery systems include greater storage capacity and quick-charge capability.

Log.   A review of original tape masters with notes referring to the order of scenes on the tapes. The VCR's foot counter or time code display registers the exact location of each shot or scene. The log also can contain useful information such as the camera move, a description of the scene such as closeup or pullback, exposure, audio quality—basically any information that will assist in the editing process.

Luminance key.   A key process based on the contrast of light and dark. For example, an object to be keyed is placed against a solid black background. The object itself has no black anywhere in its composition. Passed through the keyer all black areas are made transparent. Again video from a second source can be seen in all the places where black had been. Referencing the other extreme, the keying process could be reversed with the white or bright areas transparent rather than the black or dark.

Master.   The original recorded videotape that comes directly out of your camcorder.

Memory effect.   An inherent problem with nicad battery packs, which lose the ability to accept a full recharge over time, if the user did not fully discharge the batteries before recharging. Manufacturers tried to work around this problem by creating discharge systems, often built into the battery charger. Because of this drawback most camcorder manufacturers have switched to lithium-powered battery packs.

MIDI (music information digital interface).   A digital audio format whose files must be processed through a sound program and then on to the sound card to be heard.

Motherboard.   Home of the central processor, the heart of any computer. The motherboard also is the location for a number of muilticonnection interfaces, or "slots," used when installing dedicated circuit boards or "cards." Video cards, audio cards, controllers for disk drives, and more are installed in the slots on the motherboard.

Nonlinear editing. The new form of editing on computer. Source material from master videotapes are recorded or digitized into the computer and stored on the computer's hard drive. Scenes then can be selected and inserted into a timeline. *Nonlinear* specifically identifies the computer's ability to move scenes about at will, inserting or deleting shots and scenes at any point on the timeline.

Off-line. A low-resolution edited version of a production, not intended for distribution or viewing by a general audience.

On-line. A high-resolution edited version of a production, intended for distribution and viewing by a general audience.

Parallel port. A 25-pin interface on the back of a computer. A cable from the parallel port links the computer to peripheral hardware such as a printer or an external video capture device. With the parallel port, multiple hardware devices can be chained together, all connecting to the computer through the single connector interface.

PCI (peripheral component interconnect). One of the slots on the computer's motherboard, the location for hardware devices such as a video card.

Render. When creating an animation sequence or special effects in a nonlinear editor, the computer must calculate the pixel layout in each video frame, a process called *rendering*.

S-video. A type of video processing that keeps the color (chrominance) information separate from the contrast (luminance) information. Used on prosumer and industrial-level VCRs and camcorders, S-video delivers higher-resolution images with less color distortion.

Serial port. A multipin (9- or 25-pin) interface on the back of a computer. A cable from the serial port links the computer to peripheral hardware such as a printer or an external video capture device.

Scene. A scene is a segment of video within an edited video program with content that relates to a common time and place. A single scene can be composed of many different shots with a variety of views and angles.

Scroll. Graphics or titles that go up from the bottom of the screen such as the credits at the end of a movie.

SCSI (small computer systems interface). A high-speed interface for transferring data to and from disk drives. The SCSI card is a piece of hardware, a small circuit board, installed in the computer's PCI slot. It is linked to the disk drives via multipin ribbon cables.

Shot.   One specific recording from the camera to the tape with a starting point and ending point.

Special effects.   Dozens of types of transitions fall under the realm of special effects, ways to manipulate the video as you go from one screen to another: Squeeze, page turns, warps, and curls are just a few different types of edit special effects systems.

Storyboard.   Part of the production planning process, the storyboard is like a cartoon of the script, with visual images indicating the subject and action of each scene arranged in the proper order representing the final edit. Storyboards originally were hand-drawn pictures put on a wall but today commonly are thumbnail or miniature images arranged on a computer screen.

Straight cut.   Editing so that video scenes come one after the other, one shot or scene to the next with no transition in between.

Streaming.   The process of sending video information over the Internet. Video clips are fed to a computer a few frames at a time, while the computer's resident media player processes and displays the frames on the screen in a steady "stream," or flow of information.

Strobe.   A video special effect named after the strobe light, which blinks off and on many times a second, delivering a staggered motion of a subject to the eye. On a video screen, strobed motion removes frames from each second of a video clip, extending the view of the remaining frames by repeating them, making ordinarily fluid video appear choppy.

Sync.   Generally refers to the harmonious electronic alignment of video signals from two different sources.

Thumbnail.   A compact or miniature version representing the appearance of a larger image. In a video production, thumbnails are used to symbolize the subjects and action of a complete scene. On the Internet, thumbnails are used to deliver a quick loading representation of an image. Selecting the thumbnail prompts the loading of the image at full size.

.tif.   An image file format that allows the separation of color information as necessary for commercial printing.

Time code.   Most professional and now many prosumer camcorders record on the videotape a counter number permanently identified with each frame of video. This allows the person doing the editing to accurately locate scenes on the master tape and edit controllers to maintain frame accuracy for perfect edits.

Timeline. When editing on a nonlinear system, the timeline depicts the sequence of events or video scenes and audio soundtracks. It can be compressed or magnified in view, from fractions of a second to hours, depending on the length of the finished program. It also can deliver relevant information such as the location of transitions and special effects, titles, and the name and length of individual scenes.

Transition. The sequence from one scene to the next. In straight cuts, as the term suggests, one piece of video goes to the next with no space or segue in between. However, an editor often will use some sort of special effect as a bridge between the two adjacent segments, a transition that carries the viewer's attention from one to the other. There are many different types of transitions.

Trim. Select the In and Out points of an individual video clip. For example, if the original video clip was digitized at 15 seconds and the portion desired for the edited production is 12.5 seconds, the producer will "trim" the clip by selecting new In and Out points so that only a portion of the clip is used.

USB (universal serial bus). A relatively new connection or interface found on a computer system.

.wav. An audio file format that contains all information necessary to reproduce sound directly through a sound card.

White balance. A feature found on all video camcorders, white balance establishes the reference for color reproduction and recording. Most consumer systems perform the function automatically, however, a manual option is desirable for more color accuracy. The camera is focused on a white subject, the operator presses a button engaging the white balance processing, which determines how white should be seen.

Wipe. A type of transition, the wipe is a 2D transition: One video image is covered or "wiped" away by another. It can be horizontal from side to side, up from the bottom, or down from the top, even corner to corner. It can open up from the center in the shape of a square, a diamond, a circle, or an oval. The edges might be hard and distinct or soft and out of focus.

XLR. A balanced audio connector with three pins: a main signal, a ground, and a separate ground shield one for protecting the audio signal from picking up noise and interference. This type of connection usually is found only on commercial-, industrial-, or broadcast-quality equipment.

Y/C. The separation of the Y (contrast or luminance) and the C (color or chrominance) in S-video cables and processing.

Index

DATE DUE

GAYLORD   PRINTED IN U.S.A.